ANOTHER CRIES FOR JUSTICE

ANOTHER CRIES FOR JUSTICE

"A Personal Story about the Intentional Racial Injustice in the U.S. Courts"

By

Grady Michael Stroman

Certificate of Registration

This Certificate issued under the seal of the Copyright Office in accordance with title 17, *United States Code*, attests that registration has been made for the work identified below. The information on this certificate has been made a part of the Copyright Office records.

Marybeth Peters

Register of Copyrights, United States of America

Registration Number

TXu 1-632-461

Effective date of registration:

February 19, 2008

This book was printed in the United States of America.

Rev. date: 06/04/2013

To order additional copies of this book, contact:
Xlibris Corporation
1-888-795-4274
www.Xlibris.com
Orders@Xlibris.com

56062

Dedication

*This book is dedicated to my sons, Elijah and Tobias, so that
they will have a written document of the first fifty years of my life.
From this book they, and their children, will see life was not
always a bed of roses for me.
Also, they will know that the love for myself, and the love
from family and friends, have helped me smooth
out the rough times.*

*Additionally, this book is dedicated in loving memories of four
women: my mother Barbara, my grandmother Gertrude,
my aunt Vera, and also to my first wife Delia, who
all of them played a role in molding me into the intelligent,
strong, and proud man that I am today.*

Acknowledgment

Even though he has passed away I want to acknowledge my deepest thanks to my very dear friend, advisor, and counselor, "Aaron B. Lee," for his investigative knowledge and experience pertaining to my Title VII allegations against my ex-employer, which prepared me for the struggles I encountered in bringing my case to trial in Federal District Court in Tacoma, Washinton before the Honorable Jack E. Tanner.

I also want to acknowledge my gratitude to him for spending many hours with me in the beginning helping me set the foundation in writing my story, again I say "Thank you very much."

Also,

Thanks to Andrea "Moose" White my longest friend, for whom I have a special love, for the many hours she spent working on my book proofreading it for me after I lost Aaron.

Lastly but not least,

To Sefla Fuhrman, whom I believe was a "God send." After I had organized my thoughts for my book and put them down on paper, I felt I needed someone with more skills than both Aaron and Andrea in telling my story to the public. I met Ms. Fuhrman through her mother, Ruth, who happens to work with me as a bus driver for King County Metro. After talking to Ruth about my book that I was putting together she stated that her daughter taught high school English as a Foreign Language, and undergraduate social science courses, and I should talk to her for help. After meeting with Ms. Fuhrman she took an interest in my story. So, for seven months she worked closely with me to show me how to make my writing more clear and precise. The knowledge that I learned from her in improving my writing skills is invaluable.

CONTENTS

Preface

My story covers the first fifty years of my life. I divided the story into two parts, the first part telling the reader about my life before going into the military and my life while in the military. In the first part, I am introducing myself to the reader, so that one may see how different personal situations and living in a culture diverse environment helped mold me into the person that I am today. I believe the reader needs to know and comprehend the above so that one can understand my actions in the second and main part of my story.

The second part I talk about my experiences after leaving the military, when I decided to accept a job at a major grocery warehouse corporation in the Tacoma, WA area. I talk about how I spoke out against the status quo of racial employment discrimination at this corporation. Additionally, the struggles I encounter filing complaints with the Washington State Human Rights Commission against this corporation, and the barriers I had to overcome before I could have a federal district court trial pertaining to my complaints against this corporation. Lastly, I tell the reader about a shocking experience, which was when a philosophy contained in the *Dred Scott's case* was applied to the federal district court judge and me, by a federal appellate court reviewing my case.

Using my case as an example, my intentions are to show the ruling by the federal appellate court was based on race, and how this court perpetrated a deliberate fabrication of the truth. Furthermore, my case shows that the same federal appellate court did knowingly perpetuate this race based fabrication by making the ruling federal case law within that circuit. This means this untruthful ruling amount to inequality for individuals of color. Now with my story, individuals can see first hand, not all cases are decided according to the law, some are decided by race and deviation from the truth. Based on the above is why I titled my book "*Another Cries For Justice.*"

Chapter One

My Parents and Going to Texas

In 1954, the U.S. Supreme Court ruled in "Brown v. Board of Education" that separate but equal was no longer the law of the land, southern schools were forced to integrate "with deliberate speed." This was an important ruling because it meant that the African American children in the south would receive the same education as white children. With new opportunities for education, African Americans believed that life would be improved for them and their children.

I was born just before that decision on February 6, 1954, to Barbara Ann and Grady Michael Stroman in Riverside, California where my parents believed education and interacting with other races was the American way. My mother was raised in Mobile, Alabama where she graduated from high school at the age of sixteen. She completed two years of college by the age of eighteen. My father was raised near Houston, Texas. He did not have the formal education that my mother had. He worked as a cook for the railroad before entering the U.S. Marine Corps. My parents met while my father was in the military, and later they married. Both of them were determined that their children would have the best education and life interactions that they could give them.

My brother Ronald, who is a year and a half older than me, is the oldest. He was born by my mother before my parents met. I was the first born after my parents met. Next came my sister Phyllis who is a year and a half younger than me, and then my brother Donny who is eight years younger than me.

Growing up, we always lived on or near a Marine Corps base in the Southern California area. While living on or around a Marine Corps Base, I was exposed to families of many different races. This was great for me because the experience of being around and interacting with other races and cultures taught me how to be a positive member in an interracial society. Thanks should go to President Truman for integrating the military in 1948 when he issued Executive Order 9981.

> Because of President Truman's gutsy decision to integrate the military in 1948, in effect to do the right-thing, the U.S. military has become a paradigm of institutional racial integration. President Truman's integration of the military eventually led to the creation and passing of the 1964 Civil Rights Act, which pertained to racial discrimination in employment.[1]

I can still remember when we lived in Anaheim, California, and my father decided to take us to Texas to visit his parents and family. It was around 1961 when my father made this decision to go to Texas, mainly to see his father who was in the hospital. I can remember during our travel from California to Texas, while moving through Arizona or New Mexico that we had no concerns about our interaction with the whites with whom we met at gas stations and other places. However, when we arrived in Texas, we had to act in a different manner when it came to interacting with whites.

---

[1] The Truman Legacy: Desegregation of the Armed Forces "Military has been Desegregation Model" by Major Cox, Published August 4, 1998 (Montgomery Advertiser). Prior to this Executive Order 9981, in 1941 President Roosevelt issued Executive Order 8802 prohibiting government contractors from committing employment discrimination based on race, color, or national origin and in 1942 he issued an order allowing blacks to enlist in the Marine Corps. However, the newly enlisted black recruits were segregated from the white recruits and they did their boot camp only at Montford Point, North Carolina (these black recruits are know as the Montford Point Marines).

We were told not to talk to the white people that we met as we were used to doing in California, and as we did in Arizona and New Mexico. As a young boy, this was hard for me to understand, as I was not familiar with serious prejudice. My mother later told me it was because my parents were aware of the Emmett Till incident.[2] When we arrived in Texas, there was something that always has stayed in my mind, it was the first and only time I actually saw "white only" and "colored only" signs at some gas stations in Texas. This was in the early sixties, and one must remember that Texas was once a Confederate state. The words on those signs stuck in my head all these years, but back then I was a child so I never got what it all meant until I was older. Only then did I start to understand what I saw as a child and understood what my parents were worried about related to their children interacting with whites in Texas. After we arrived in Bay City, Texas, we headed to my grandmother's house. Bay City was a little town with many small old houses that were sitting on concrete blocks. While visiting with my grandmother, I remember asking her where the bathroom was. She looked at me and said "outback". I thought everybody had a bathroom in his or her house. I looked at my father and asked him what she was talking about. He said, "Yes, the bathroom is outback," and he could tell that I was totally confused, so he took me outback to show me. As I looked at this old wooden outhouse, I noticed that every house around me had one of these in the back yard. I also remember visiting with my grandmother and my aunt Manie Jean for a while before going to my grandfather and uncle's homes in Houston.

---

[2]   Emmett Till was a Negro boy from Chicago who was murdered at the age of 14 in Mississippi in 1955 for flirting with a white woman (he winked at her) while he was visiting relatives in Mississippi.

My grandfather's house was a lot different from my grandmother's because it had a bathroom in the house and a big yard for us to play in. My grandfather had a trucking business, and he employed several drivers; I remember thinking that he seemed to be financially secure. He also had a wife who was a lot younger than he was and, as I remember, she was nice looking. They had a son by the name of Kenneth who was my uncle and about my age. I recall playing with him around the house and the neighborhood. We played games like tag, football, and hide and seek with the other black kids in his neighborhood. The other children asked me why I talked like white folks. Because I was raised in a multi-racial environment, my speech was different from theirs. Nevertheless, we would go to the neighborhood market that was owned and run by a black family and hang out there drinking 'soda water' (from Kenneth and these other children, I learned to call a soft drink "soda water" instead of "soda pop"). Additionally, from them I started drinking Royal Crown soda and not Coca-Cola, and instead of saying "you guys," I began using "y'all." I also remember telling Kenneth about the outhouse that I saw at my grandmother's house. This was no big thing to him because he was used to seeing them throughout his childhood.

Besides Kenneth, my father had three other younger brothers, who were closer to his age, Johnny Jr., Eugene, and J.B. and all three were rodeo riders. One of my uncles, J.B., had a horse that he kept at my grandfather's home by the name of Coco, and my uncle would let us ride him around my grandfather's house. I can remember going to another one of my uncle's homes, Eugene, where he had a riding ring. My father told me that this is where my uncles rode wild horses and made them tame so that others could ride them.

Before we left my grandfather's home, I remember going to visit my grandfather in the hospital. I cannot remember what was wrong with him, but it was bad. I also remember my mother and my grandfather's wife taking us kids (Ronald, Phyllis, Kenneth, and me) to Galvin, Texas to spend an afternoon at the beach. From what I remember the beach was different from the beach, our family went to in Anaheim. At this beach, I remember the water was warmer, the beach was not that crowded, and we were able to walk out much further than the beach that we went to in the Anaheim.

A few days later after the beach outing, I remember that my parents took Phyllis, Ronald, and me on a family outing to Juarez, Mexico to buy gifts for our relatives in Texas. The mid day morning that we got into the family's car to go to Juarez was a nice and clear morning. When we arrived at the border between the U.S. and Mexico, I remember we parked our car on the U.S. side and walked through a gate where a sign said, "You are now in Mexico." We walked along this dirt road for a short period of time, and then we were in Juarez. I remember one of the first things that we did was get a family picture of all of us sitting on a wooden cart that had two burros hitched to it, and each of the burros had a sombrero on their head where one had the word Juarez and the other had the word Mexico.

While we walked around looking for gifts at the many vendors along the streets, I was looking in the different store windows at the Mexican cowboy clothes (the Spanish word for cowboy is vaquero or caballero). This was the first time that I saw leather and suede pants, which were on different mannequins in the windows. I really liked the way they looked with silver buttons along the outer seam that covered the boots—the silver buttons were called conchos—these pants also had matching short jackets. I even saw saddles that were spectacularly outfitted with silver and fancy leather designs. During the times with my uncles in Texas, I never saw any of them having any of this kind of stuff. Since then I have always said to myself if I am ever able, I am going to look like these mannequins and my horse will have a nice saddle like the ones I saw in Juarez.

When it was time for us to go we walked the same way as we did getting there, but when we arrived at the border my father had to show his military identification card for us to return to the U.S. side of the border. It was easier going across the border then than compared to what one has to go through nowadays. However, to me this was a nice family outing that I have never forgotten. When it was time to leave my grandfather's house to go back to California, I can still remember my father saying, "While driving through Texas, we still have to be careful until we get out of the state." Those few days seeing and experiencing what I did stayed with me all my life.

Back in Anaheim, California, my life continued as it was before. We lived about seven blocks from Disneyland, and my father was stationed at El Toro Marine Corps Air Station Base. My father also moonlighted as a cook at the Disneyland Hotel on his off days from his military duties. My mother kept up the home and took care of us. I guess many kids at that time would think living so close to Disneyland was the neatest place to live. I must admit that it was nice to be able to go to Disneyland whenever my parents wanted to take us. In addition, it helped that my father worked there, so he was able to get tickets for us to ride any of the rides at Disneyland no matter how many times we wanted to. I remember I always wanted to drive the motorized cars and go on the submarine ride more than any other rides.

I remember the neighborhood being integrated—with both white and Mexican families—but where I went to school my sister Phyllis and I were the only African Americans in our classes. She was in the first grade and I was in the second grade. Actually, I believe we were the only African American family in our neighborhood. We did most of our shopping on El Toro Marine Corps Air Station Base Commissary and the PX. In addition, while on the base, Ronald and I would get our hair cut with my father while my mother and my sister Phyllis would do the shopping at the Commissary. Afterwards, we all would eat hamburgers with French fries. About a year after our trip to Texas my youngest brother Donny was born.

In 1963, we moved from Anaheim just before I started the third grade. I can only remember going to school there for one year, and before that we lived in Lake Elsinore where I remember going to kindergarten and first grade with my cousin Norma-Gene. After Anaheim, we moved to Camp Pendleton Marine Corps Base in Oceanside, California. I went to school on the base for third, fourth, and part of my fifth grade years. When we moved to Camp Pendleton, it was the first time I ever remember seeing and interacting with Samoans and Asians. I got along with them just as well as the whites and Mexicans in Anaheim. While living on Camp Pendleton Base the only colors that mattered were the Marine Corps colors. While living on the base everybody was like a big family and race played no part in that environment. I also remember the assassination of President Kennedy in 1963, and the passing of General Douglas MacArthur in 1964, both of these were major incidents for anyone living on a military base. The few years I spent living on Camp Pendleton were pertinent years in my young life—they led me on a path to who I am today through the people I met and the friends that I made. During these years, I realized how important family and friends would become. My life was starting to change and take its shape.

Chapter Two

Life Before My Parent's Divorce

After Camp Pendleton, in the summer of 1964 we moved into the house our parents bought in Oceanside, California. Our house was on the Eastside of Oceanside where most of the Blacks, Mexicans, and Samoans lived; most of the families were connected with the military. In this neighborhood, there were a lot of children to play with, and the main playtime activities were playing different sports. I started playing organized baseball when I was about eight years old while we lived on Camp Pendleton Base. I played in the outfield because I liked catching and running after fly balls. After moving to Oceanside, I still played organized baseball, but now I played for a team that was part of Oceanside Little League. 'Mission Square' was the name of our team, named for a shopping center in Oceanside. I started playing first base for this team in my fifth and sixth grade years. In my seventh and eighth grade years (1966-67), I did not play organized baseball because my father served in Vietnam, and I decided to stay around the house with my mother. This was my father's first tour in Vietnam. However, I still played sports around the neighborhood, ran track and got involved with lifting weights at the Boy's Club in Oceanside.

I can also remember that while in fifth grade, my mother was working at a department store by the name of W.T. Grant, which was in the Mission Square Shopping Center. W.T. Grant was a major department store chain with many stores throughout the southern California area. I liked going into the department store and seeing my mother, who was one of the only two African American ladies who worked there, helping customers shop at the store. My mother had two years of college; she took classes related to being a secretary, which included classes in short hand. My mother knew she was qualified for a position for which she had applied as a secretary with W.T. Grant. During those days in the early 1960's, a good secretary had to know short hand. When my mother applied for this secretary position, I can remember her being deeply involved with the National Association for the Advancement of Colored People (N.A.A.C.P.), and I can remember her telling me about the 1964 Civil Rights Act outlawing racial discrimination in the workplace that was signed into law by President Johnson in July of 1964.

My mother made allegations of job discrimination based on race, according to the 1964 Civil Rights Act, against W.T. Grant when they hired a white woman who my mother believed was less qualified than she was. During the investigation of my mother's allegations, my mother and W.T. Grant agreed upon a settlement pertaining to her allegations. I do not remember what my mother and W.T. Grant agreed upon, but I do know that my mother decided to accept a position with another big department store (Value Fair) in Oceanside as an office secretary. Yes, my mother was the first African American woman that I ever saw working in an office position as a secretary in Oceanside, and this was sometime in 1965. My grandmother, my aunt, and all the rest of the family were proud of my mother's success. My mother accepted this secretarial position before my father left for his first tour of duty in Vietnam in 1966.

My father's first tour of duty in Vietnam was in 1966, and he returned home around the end of 1967. When my father came home, those were happy times for our family. I can remember everything was fine between my parents. We would go on family outings to the San Diego Zoo, Disneyland, Knott's Berry Farm, and the Del Mar fair. I also remember my parents' friends coming over to listen to music and dance at our house. I also remember spending Christmas time with my relatives and friends at each other's homes. A few months later, sometime in 1968 when I was still in junior high school my father had to go back to Vietnam. Because he received wounds while in Vietnam during this tour, he came back, and I specifically remember this because I had not yet started high school. By this time, my father had spent close to twenty years in the Marine Corps where he did tours of duty in the Korean War as well as in Vietnam. For his service in each war, my father received a Purple Heart Medal, which is a significant honor that is given to military personnel who have been wounded, or killed, in combat while defending the U.S. Constitution[3]. The rights contained in the U.S. Constitution, which all military personnel defend, are supposed to be afforded to all citizens of this nation, regardless of race.

When he came home after his second tour of Vietnam, my mother told my father about a neighbor who had been coming by the house while he was in Vietnam—a person he knew from both the neighborhood and the military. I can remember the neighbor coming by to talk to my mother, but my mother never considered him any more than a family friend. I do not know exactly what happened after my mother told my father this, but afterwards he retired from the Marine Corps. Looking back, I now believe because my mother was always being complimented on her beauty and grace—she was a strikingly beautiful light skinned black woman—is the reason why my father did not want to leave her alone while he was in Vietnam being a Marine; plus he had fulfilled his twenty years requirement for retirement. Later I will talk about my father's inability to leave my mother alone, which drove her away from

---

[3] There are also two other avenues whereby it is authorized for a military person to receive the Purple Heart Medal.

him, and his actions that killed any love we had for him one Easter Sunday morning.

I remember after he retired he worked for the City of Oceanside as a bus driver, when I was in the eighth grade. I also remember him being a part-time school bus driver at Oceanside High School in my freshman year at the same high school. During this time, I recall that my father drank a lot, and he and my mother frequently fought physically. Before his second tour of Vietnam, I do not remember these things happening. Now that I am an adult and know how a relationship between a man and a woman can be, I see how my parents' marriage started to go downwards when my mother told my father about the neighbor. In any event, my parents separated and my mother, brothers, and sister moved to an apartment close to my grandmother and my Aunt Vera's house on the eastside of Oceanside; this was in the early part of 1969.

While living at this apartment, I remember my father would harass my mother by threatening to take back the family car so that she could not go back and forth to work at Value Fair. He would also call her continually just to argue, and he displayed other negative behavior that drove my mother farther away from him. It got to the point that my mother told my father he could have the family car back and she would walk to and from work. My mother was true to her word. She walked about three miles each way to and from work to show that she could make it without my father's help. My mother was around thirty-four years old when this happened. She eventually divorced my father late in 1969.

Before my parents divorce, I also remember taking an interest in individuals like Dr. Martin Luther King Jr. and groups like the Black Panthers, and talking to the older young black males in the neighborhood about racism and the military. I can remember how sad my mother and many other African American ladies were when Dr. Martin Luther King Jr. was murdered in 1968. I also remember the killing of Black Panthers throughout the Southern California area because they had the courage to expose the racism by the police in the State of California. I remember the Black Power movement at the 1968 Summer Olympics when Tommie Smith and John Carlos gave their black power salutes on the victory stand. The black power salutes were part of a movement led by Harry Edwards, called the "Revolt of the Black Athlete."[4] The times between 1968 and 1971 were violent years for me with a killing that changed my world forever, and in 1972 a tragedy that took away my best friend.

---

[4]   "The Revolt of the Black Athlete" by Harry Edwards, Published 1970.

Chapter Three

The Killing of My Mother and
The Death of My Best Friend

From the divorce proceedings, my mother was award the house in late 1969, so my father moved out, and my mother with her children moved back into our house. Even after the divorce, we still did not have a car, and my mother now had to walk five miles each way back and forth to work to pay the mortgage on the house. When I was sixteen that summer of 1970, I started working at Von's Grocery Store as a box boy after school and nights. I felt good about earning my own money and working for this major grocery store chain. Sometimes my father would come to see me there, and we would talk for a while at the check out stand. I was saving most of my money so that I could buy a car to be able to take my mother back and forth to work.

I remember my mother and I went looking for cars at car lots in Oceanside. At each car lot, I would look at the fast running cars with big engines, and she would look at the good reliable family cars. My mother got her way, and we used my money as the down payment on a 1964 Chevy four door Bel-Air. The first and only car that my mother had after her divorce from my father was the car that she and I bought together. By this time, my mother had been working in her secretary position for almost five or six years, and she seemed to be enjoying her job.

Then, on Easter Sunday, 1971, my father came to our house and wanted to take my brother Donny to Disneyland. I think Donny was around eight years old. My mother answered the door when my father came to our house to get Donny. Donny asked if his cousin Lee could also go, but my father said no. Donny then said that he did not want to go if his cousin Lee could not go with them. My mother and father started to argue about Donny not wanting to go and then my father pulled out a small pistol and shot my mother several times in her chest. I was awakened by screaming, crying, and pounding on the garage door by my sister Phyllis. I had turned the garage into my bedroom so that I could have privacy when my friends came to visit me. When I came running out of the garage, I saw my brother Ronald across the street hitting my father as he was attempting to drive away. I ran over to where Ronald was to find out what was going on. Ronald told me that our father had just shot our mother. I reached in the car, opened the car door, and pulled my father out. While I had my father pinned up against the car, holding him so that he could not leave, he somehow shot me in the leg causing me to let him go. Ronald started running away from the area, and my father then fired three shots at Ronald missing all three times. I ran back to our house to see what Ronald was talking about, and as I ran through the front door, I heard Phyllis and Donny crying in terror, and then I saw my mother lying in a pool of blood. I then began looking for my father's 30/30 rifle that we kept at our house. When I found the rifle and bullets, I ran out of the house believing that I could catch up with my father before he left the neighborhood. I wanted to shoot him.

As I was running down the street with the rifle, an Oceanside police officer was driving up the street to investigate this reported shooting. The officer was the one who patrolled the neighborhood for years, and he would talk to the kids in the neighborhood when we were in the street playing. On this morning, when he saw me running with the rifle towards him, he stopped his police car in the middle of the street, got out of his car and pulled out his gun. He told me that if I did not stop running, and did not drop the weapon, he would shoot me. I did what he said, and he put me in the back seat of his police car. The officer then ran to our house, saw my mother, and radioed for an ambulance; however, an ambulance was already on the way. While in the police car, the officer told me that he had just received a call pertaining to a shooting. When he saw me running down the street with the rifle is why he pulled his gun on me. As I watched from the inside of the police car, the ambulance came and took my mother to the hospital. When the police officer came to let me out of the back seat of the police car, he saw that I had been shot and that I was bleeding from my leg. He took me to the emergency room at the same hospital where the ambulance had taken my mother. On the way to the hospital, he said that he was sorry that he had said he would shoot me, and that if he had known what my father had done, he would have let me go after him.

At the hospital, I was in the same room with my mother but on the other side of a partition from where the doctors were operating on my mother. When a different doctor came in to see about me, I heard the other doctors who were operating on my mother say that my mother was dead. I heard them say it was from internal bleeding that they could not stop. I cannot explain the hurt that I felt at that moment, the emptiest feeling knowing that my mother would no longer be with us. Yes, I can describe the hurt and pain that I felt because as I am writing this I can feel the hurt and pain that I experienced then. It feels like something is pulling on my heart making my chest area hurt and it is hard to breathe. Now uncontrollable tears start rolling down my face and the more I try to control these tears the more I feel I cannot breathe. I also remember after this hurt the mental agony of hoping this was just a bad dream and my mother was really alive and still with us. Then reality set in and I felt hatred towards my father as I never felt before and wished that he had been killed in Vietnam.

After the death of my mother, the State of California wanted to take custody of Ronald and Donny. Ronald was mentally retarded, and Donny was only eight years old. My father was being held in jail for the murder of my mother. The State of California thought at first that a foster home would be the best place for them. Instead, the State gave custody of all of us to my aunt Vera. We moved in with my aunt Vera, who also lived on the eastside of Oceanside. My aunt Vera got custody of us because she and my grandmother fought the State so that the system would not separate my mother's children from each other. In addition, my aunt Vera and my grandmother were not going to let this happen, because for the majority of our lives my family lived close to my grandmother and my mother's younger sister Vera and her family.

The only time I can remember that we did not live blocks from my grandmother and aunt was when we lived in Anaheim. During this time, my grandmother's family, my Aunt Vera's family, and other relatives lived in Lake Elsinore about an hour's drive East of Anaheim. Besides my mother and my aunt Vera, my grandmother had two other children: my aunt Jackie who was three years older than me, and my uncle Gary who was three years younger than I was. My Aunt Vera and her husband Allen had five children: my cousin Terry, who was two years younger than me; my cousins Lee and Barbara (the twins) who were a year older than Donny was; and my cousins Kate and Toby who were just babies. Since we all lived close to each other for the majority of our lives, we were like one big family with my grandmother presiding over us as the "Matriarch." Because of all this family love we had, it was natural that my grandmother and my Aunt Vera would fight so hard to keep us together as a family. When we moved in with my Aunt Vera and her children, they lived in a small two bedroom duplex. My aunt Vera gave up the little comforts that she had so that all of her sister's children could stay within the family. She loved us all very much. All nine of us lived in this small duplex for two years, and we felt loved.

The day finally came when my father had to go to trial; both my sister and I had to testify about what happened on that Easter Sunday when my father showed up with that gun at our house. My father was found guilty and was sent to prison for the murder of my mother. We could not believe that he got such a short prison sentence of just seven years. The reason for the sentence was tied to my father's two tours in Vietnam. He pleaded temporary insanity at the time of the shooting. I vowed on that day that I would never put my children through such tragedy, that I would never be possessive or jealous about a woman like my father was, and that I would show my wife the love and respect that I showed my mother. The short time I had my mother in my life I felt proud to say, "She is my mother," and the pride of being her son laid a good foundation for me because even though she is gone I still try to make her feel proud that I am her son.

Months after my graduation from high school in 1972, another tragedy struck in my life. This was when my best friend in the world died. A couple of years after the death of my mother, I lost my friend, Lamar Ray, when he drowned surfing with some friends. I met Lamar when I was in the eighth grade, and he was a freshman in high school. His mother and father moved into a house that was just around the corner from where my family lived on the Eastside of Oceanside. Before we became friends, I can remember seeing him coming home from school. He had to go past our house to get to his. He looked like a light-skinned black preppie student. He wore corduroy pants, tan hush puppy shoes, white socks, and plaid shirts like the college prep students I saw at our high school in the late sixties. At that time he was the only child in his household, his dad was a Non-Commissioned Officer in the Marine Corps and his mother was working in the medical field as a nurse. So he had it pretty well, all things considered.

In my eighth grade year, I had a paper route, and I delivered the local newspaper throughout our neighborhood. Because I delivered the newspaper to Lamar's parents, I came to know both Lamar and his parents. I remember his mother was somewhat tall and very quiet, but his dad was very large and loud. To me, his dad was "cool" because he would stop and talk to me when he saw me delivering the newspaper or when I would come once a month to collect for the newspaper. In addition, when he drove one of his nice cars in the neighborhood, he would always drive slowly in a cool-looking kind of way. I really liked Lamar's parents, and after I lost my mother, his parents let me know that I was always welcome at their home.

Before the death of my mother, Lamar and I started talking to each other, but it took a while for us to become friends because I think he thought he was 'too good' and he was older than I was. I remember we started talking more to each other after he bought a brand new Yamaha motorcycle. Lamar was a sophomore in high school then, because that was the earliest that he could have gotten his license to operate the motorcycle on the streets of Oceanside. He was the first kid in the neighborhood to have a motorcycle, and the fact that he had a brand new one made him even more special. During this time, he had a job working at a major grocery store in Oceanside—the name of the grocery store was Mayfair Market—that was located close to the beach and close to the area in Oceanside where a lot of the preppie white students and surfers lived. This job enabled Lamar to save up his money to buy the motorcycle.

During my freshman year in high school, I do not remember seeing that much of Lamar at school, and it was not until I was a sophomore that I started seeing more of him there. I can remember seeing him walking around the high school with white preppie students going to and from classes. It seems that Lamar had many white friends; it might have been from the college prep classes that he took, or working near the beach, or maybe because of his good looks. I began to see Lamar more at school, but we did not start hanging out with each other until my junior year and his senior year in high school. We were both on the high school wrestling team, so I started going to different parties with him and his friends. I had good times at these parties. During this time, my grades started to get better, which was because Lamar told me to take school more seriously. During my junior and senior years, Lamar and I spent a lot of time together, at Wayne's house. Wayne was our Samoan friend, who also lived on the Eastside. Our Spanish friend John lived down the street from Wayne's where we all spent time hanging out, listening to music, partying and listening to Wayne, John and others playing their guitars. Wayne and John were in the same grade as Lamar and all three of them graduated from high school together.

In my senior year of high school, and Lamar's first year at Mira Costa Jr. College, we spent a lot of time together: going to concerts throughout the Southern California area; making trips to Tijuana to party all-night; hanging out at the beach with friends; and racing against other guys on the freeways around Oceanside. Also during this time, I met and started dating Delia, and by the summer of that year, we had been dating for six or seven months.

On the summer day that Lamar drowned, Delia and I were at the beach swimming, near the same area where Lamar was surfing. On that particular day, there was a strong undertow that pulled on Delia and me as we swam; both of us were caught up in it. I was lucky enough to have just enough strength to fight the undertow and make my way back to the beach. However, it took Delia about a quarter of a mile further out to sea. All I could do was watch once I got back on the beach. In the area where we were, there were no lifeguards on duty. After a while, Delia was able to swim back to shore but she was further north from where we were swimming. After hugging her, I asked her what happened. She said that we were caught in an undertow, and she said the best thing to do was just to go with the ocean current. I told her, "Well, that wasn't for me." She said that the ocean current would only take you out to sea a little way, and then you will be able to swim parallel to the shore for a few feet to get out of its pull. Once you were out of the undertow, you could ride the surf safely back to shore, which is what I did.

Delia showed me that she did not just come to the beach to tan; she also knew the ocean. Later that day after leaving the beach, Delia and I were on our way to her father's house. At that time, she was still living with her father. We saw John driving on one of the main streets by Delia's father's house. He stopped and told me that Lamar had been out surfing with Wayne and other friends. He said that Lamar had drowned. He also told me that later that night, there was a search and rescue party planned to look for Lamar's body. At first, I did not believe what John was telling me, so I told Delia that I was dropping her off at her father's house and that I was going to Wayne's house to find out what happened. After learning from Wayne that what John had said was true, I went to Lamar's house to share my grief with his parents. I told them that I would go to the beach that night and look for Lamar. We did not find Lamar's body that night. The lifeguards said the ocean would probably wash his body to shore in the morning because of the undertow. The next morning, Lamar's body was found not far from where he was last seen.

Because Lamar was well like in high school, in the different communities in North San Diego County, and at Mira Costa Jr. College he had a large funeral. His parents selected as pallbearers Lamar's close friends: Wayne, John, his white high school friends Ron and Rick, his dad's younger brother Nathaniel, and me. Delia also attended the funeral with me, our friend Angie, as well as my friend K.T. I can remember Lamar's funeral hurting me as much as I was hurting during my mother's funeral. In fact, as I am writing this, I still feel the hurt and pain from both of their deaths. Lamar was buried at the same cemetery in Oceanside as my mother was, and not far from her gravesite.

Many times when I visit my mother's gravesite, I also go and visit Lamar's. I wish both of them could have been a part of my life longer, or on this earth longer, but that was not the way God planned it, and I have to accept this bitter pill.

Chapter Four

My Years with Delia

In my junior year of high school and after the death of my mother, I started getting really good at football and other sports, like wrestling and karate. Based on my desire for recognition as a football star, in the summer of my senior year, I started taking better care of my body. I started running and lifting weights. However, my senior year football team did not do very well. Nevertheless, I did learn that it took hard work and dedication to be a good running back if I wanted to advance in football. Even though the football team did not do well, the wrestling team did very well that year, and we were the number one team in San Diego County. I was the top wrestler in my weight class in North San Diego and second in all of San Diego County. Because I did so well wrestling in the all San Diego County Tournament, this qualified me to go to the State of California Tournament. Despite my natural abilities, my heart and desire was simply not in wrestling, so I did not go to the State Wrestling Finals. Football was my passion, not wrestling.

Now let me tell you how I came to fall in love with beautiful Delia, who is half-Persian and half white. We started dating in the month of February of 1972, when I was a senior and she was a freshman in high school. We met at a party, months before we started seeing each other, where she was with a friend of both of ours, Angie. Delia and I did not get serious about each other until the summer after I graduated from high school in 1972. That summer Andrea, Linda, and Delia used to spend a lot of time at the beach together keeping their beautiful tans looking good. Each day I could not wait to see how golden brown Delia had gotten from laying out at the beach. By and by, and more and more, I fell in love with Delia. During the years I was dating Delia, I also developed a mother-son type of bond with

Delia's mother Katia. Katia was petite and a classy good-looking Persian woman. I loved and respected Katia as a son would respect and love his mother. I will never forget the times before Delia and I married and then again after our divorce, when Katia and I would just sit at her kitchen table and talk about life and the struggles the both of us were facing. I loved Katia and will always remember her, and I know that we were like mother and son up until her death in 2005. In the years from 1972 to 1976, being with Delia, Katia, and Bob (Katia's man), I was able to experience how upper income families lived on the other side of town.

Being around Bob at that time was good for me, because I believed I was the first black person in his life, and when I was with him, he always treated me with respect. He showed me that a rich white man could be good to a poor black teenager. It may have been that Bob was just a good man and would have shown the same treatment toward anyone else. I also got along with Bob's older children, Robert and Karen. They both were older than Delia and I, and we would go to parties with them. Karen was special because she was sort of like a hippie, and I could always go to her house, sit around, and talk to her about life.

Because of Delia, I was accepted in the neighborhood where Bob and Katia lived. The white friends who would come to visit the both of them on holidays also accepted me. Additionally, I was accepted at the places where they took Delia and me, for example water skiing and nice restaurants around the Oceanside and Carlsbad area. I had no problem being the only black person there. The interaction with these upper income white people taught me to be honest and real with them in our conversations and in my relationships with them.

Bob also had a neighbor who was about the same age as Robert and Karen. His name was Danny, and his wife was Kristy. Danny and Kristy both grew up in Oceanside and Danny was a life-long surfer, the type one might see in the old surfer movies. I looked up to him like an older brother. Just like Karen, I could talk to him about my deepest concerns, and he would give me advice on issues of which he had knowledge. We spent many hours in his garage playing darts, or ping-pong, or I would just watch him working on something in his garage. Danny and Bob were the ones who taught me how to water ski, and Danny tried to teach me surfing too. He was an excellent surfer in the Southern California area, but I think he realized, as well as I, that surfing was harder for me to learn than water skiing. I will always remember those days with Danny.

From a myriad of experiences in my youth, I learned how to interact with individuals of many different races and cultures, such as growing up on Marine Corps Bases in the southern California area. The time that I spent with Delia, Katia, and Bob gave me the opportunity to experience being around a life style and income level that I know I would not have experienced if not for them. These experiences helped shape the man that I would later become.

Now I want to talk about my years at Mira Costa Jr. College surrounding my football experience, and the life that Delia and I experienced while together after my senior year in high school. At the end of my senior year in high school, my Aunt Vera and all of us moved out of the small duplex on the Eastside into a house that my Aunt Vera bought in Oceanside in an area that we call the "Valley." This area was near the rear gate of Camp Pendleton Marine Corps Base. During the start of my first year at

Mira Costa Jr. College, I moved out on my own into an apartment with two teammates from the football team. One was recruited from a New Jersey high school, and the other was recruited from New York to play football at Mira Costa Jr. College. I really did not excel in football until I got to Mira Costa Jr. College. At Mira Costa Jr. College, I was part of a winning program for two years. The team played in the State of California Jr. College Championship semi final game the first year and the State Championship game my second year. Each of those years, I was one of the starting running backs, and I received State recognition based on my football accomplishments in my second year. I will never forget the friends that I made during my high school and Mira Costa Jr. College years; the life long friends like K.T., Kathy, John, Andrea (who also goes by the name Moose), Ronnie, Linda, and Frank. The memories of running the streets, partying throughout North San Diego County, and going to the different nightclubs in Tijuana with them still remain with me.

K.T. and I became friends when we were juniors in high school, even though we had known each other since we were freshmen. In my junior year, we became friends because he was a friend of Lamar's. In addition, when I started dating Delia in my senior year, he also started dating Angie. K.T. did not date Angie too long because he met Kathy, and he started dating her. This was after the summer K.T. and I had gradated from high school, and I was now in my first year at Mira Costa Jr. College. Kathy lived in the apartments across the street from the apartments where John was living. John and K.T. had known each other for years when their families lived in military housing on Camp Pendleton Base. The apartment that I lived in was around the corner from the different apartments where Kathy and John lived, and I used to go over to John's apartment to party, play chess, and hang out.

When I met Kathy, I used to see K.T. going over to Kathy mother's apartment to see Kathy, and she would sometimes come over to John's apartment. Thus, I also befriended Kathy, and her good friend Carol (who she called her sister), and John and I spent a lot of time talking and hanging out with them. During this time, John and I became closer friends, and after I left Mira Costa Jr. College in 1974, we rented a house together over on the Eastside sometime in 1975.

At that time, John, K.T., and I were working at the Camp Pendleton Commissary bagging groceries for tips. We made decent money bagging groceries in those days. My friend, Andrea started hanging out with us during this time. I knew Andrea before I knew K.T. and John because she lived on the Eastside when my mother was still alive. My friend Walter, brought Andrea and a girlfriend of hers over to my house one night in 1969, when my bedroom was in the garage, to hang out and listen to music, and talk before my mother ran the girls out of my room. Andrea and I remained friends over the years. During the time that John and I lived together, Delia, Andrea, Kathy, K.T., John, Linda, Frank and I used to go to parties, concerts, nightclubs together in the San Diego and Orange County area (the girls had fake IDs so that they could get in), and nightclubs in Tijuana (the girls did not need to have fake IDs in Mexico).

Around this time, K.T. and I would go to my Uncle Al's house in Long Beach, where we would hang out with my uncle Al. In addition, K.T. and I would go exploring different nightclubs around the Long Beach area and afterwards we frequently would spend the night at my Uncle Al's house. Over the years after my mother's death, and after the divorce between my aunt Vera and my uncle Al, I maintained a close relationship with my uncle Al and even today, we still remain close. We developed a loving relationship throughout the years, where he would always talk to me as if I were his son and he always tried to guide me in the right direction. I guess this was natural since he had known me for almost my entire life. Even back then, I knew if I had any sons I would have a relationship with them similar to the one that I had with my uncle Al, through loving, caring, and open communication.

Over thirty years later, every time I go back to Oceanside, I spend time with both K.T. and John, whom I love like brothers. Andrea (Moose) and Kathy, also remain dear to me. Throughout the years, K.T., Kathy, John, Andrea, and I have been together through the good times and the bad times. We all have been there for each other in times of the loss of loved ones.

Because of my grades, I did not go to a four-year college after Mira Costa Jr. College, mainly because I was still out running around in the streets. I started looking for a job so that Delia and I could start a life together. I could not find a job that paid enough to start a family in Oceanside so at the age of twenty-two, and after talking it over with Delia, I decided that I would enlist in the Army. My duty station would be Fort Lewis, Washington. After basic training, I returned to Oceanside where Delia and I were married. We had a small ceremony in the same church where my mother's funeral service took place years earlier. Our close friends Andrea, John, and K.T. were part of the wedding party, and Katia and other friends attended the service. My grandmother also attended Delia and my wedding, and based on my grandmother's feelings towards Delia she especially welcomed Delia into our family. A couple of days after our wedding service, I returned to Fort Lewis alone so that I could find an apartment, hopefully in a good area of Tacoma where Delia and I could live. After arriving at Fort Lewis in February of 1977, I was surprised to see the number of inter-racial marriages and blended children from those marriages at Fort Lewis and in the Tacoma area. Since Delia and I formed an inter-racial couple, I assumed we would be accepted there.

Chapter Five

My Year on Fort Lewis' Semi-Pro Football Team

After Delia and I settled into our apartment in Tacoma, which was the spring or early summer of 1977, I can still remember Delia tanning on our second story apartment balcony. We would also go out to the different nightclubs in Tacoma and concerts in Seattle. My sister Phyllis, her husband Clarence, and their son C.T. were already living in Portland, Oregon before I enlisted in the military. My sister and her family would drive up to visit with Delia and me, as often as Delia and I would drive down to Portland to visit with them.

Additionally, during this time, I started concentrating on getting ready to compete for the Fort Lewis football team. I liked the fact that there were military personnel from various parts of the U.S. who would be competing against me for a running back position; I was really looking forward to this challenge. When the day finally arrived for the competition to begin, I was surprised to see some old Samoan friends, Buck and Vaa. We grew up in Oceanside together and knew each other well from our neighborhood and from playing sports. After saying our hellos, I went with the individuals who were trying out for a running back position. Based on my height and weight, some of those individuals suggested that I should be with the linemen, I just laughed at that idea. The majority of the team was surprised when they saw me working out in military boots, i.e. running pass patterns, running stairs, and running around the track. Again, I just laughed at them when they made their comments and said, "Just watch, once we start running plays." The military boots were heavier than my football shoes so my legs became stronger and my stride faster and farther. I learned this trick from the ex-marines I competed against while at Mira Costa College. Before our first game, I had proven that I was the biggest, strongest, and one of the fastest running backs on the team, based on my natural abilities and method of training.

At our first game, which was a home game at Fort Lewis, I scored two touchdowns, and had over 100 yards of rushing, and about 50 yards receiving. My Samoan friends from Oceanside were also starting at their positions on the team. Buck was the starting quarterback, and Vaa was the starting middle linebacker. Here is a short history of both of them. Buck was about four years older than me, and after playing for Oceanside High School football, he went to Utah State University where he played as a quarterback. After Utah State University, the Green Bay Packers drafted him as a quarterback. After a year or two with the Packers, he came back to Oceanside where he held odd jobs before going into the Army. Vaa and I met in high school in our freshman year while we both were on the Oceanside High School football team. He started as middle linebacker all four years we played football together. I saw Vaa mainly at the beach surfing with other Samoans and whites, and at Lamar's Samoan friend Wayne's house playing the guitar when I hung out with Lamar. He and Buck went into the Army together as Rangers. So it was by chance (or luck) that all of us ended up being at Fort Lewis trying out for the same football team.

I did well that 1977 season, where I gained over twelve hundred yards of total offense in eight games. I received national honors as a running back in the semi-pro leagues, and was voted the most valuable player on the Fort Lewis football team. At the end of the season, the team had a banquet to hand out awards and trophies. I could not attend the banquet to accept the trophy for most valuable player, but my friend Buck accepted the trophy for me. I could not attend the banquet because a few days before the banquet I was told that my father had died in a trucking accident. After his prison sentence for killing my mother, he started driving trucks in the greater Los Angles area. I learned about this after his death because up to this time I did not want anything to do with him. Anyhow, my commanding officer called me, at Delia's and my apartment, to tell me that I needed to get in touch with the Red Cross Office on Fort Lewis immediately. This was during the winter of 1977 because Delia and I were living in a different apartment just outside of Fort Lewis and I can remember snow on our cars.

I called the Red Cross Office where they informed me that my father had died in a trucking accident in California and I was excused from duty to take care of the funeral arrangements. Because I was named next of kin, I had to identify his body, plus I was the only one named on his insurance policies to pay for his funeral arrangements. Because my father killed my mother I really did not want anything to do with his funeral arrangements, but after I talked to my grandmother, my aunt Vera, and my uncle Al they all convinced me that I should do this out of respect for my mother, and, he was my father. So at the age of 23, I, my sister Phyllis, and my brother Donny buried our father, without shedding a tear over him, in a cemetery in the Los Angles area near his then girlfriend's home, and near her family who got to know him and grew to like him after he came out of prison. By burying him in the Los Angles cemetery, I knew he was away from where our mother was buried. I was glad this horrible chapter in my life had come to an end, but it would be years before I could also bury my hatred toward him, though I finally did.

It was great being on the same team with my Samoan brothers from home, showing our football skills that we had developed in Oceanside, and forming an even closer relationship with each other. Even though I had some good times playing football, Delia and I started to drift apart. I will accept most of the blame for our break-up, but I have to say that Delia's refusal to let her employer know that she was married to a black man had something to do with our break-up. After we moved to Tacoma, Delia got a job as a waitress at this nice, white owned restaurant near the corner of 38th street and Pacific Avenue. Delia would tell me that she was afraid that she might lose her job if management found out that she was married to me. Delia did not want anyone from the restaurant to see us together, so I had to pick her up or drop her off for work behind the building in the alley. I could not go into the restaurant to wait for her to get off work. Delia acted differently in Tacoma than she did in Oceanside. In Oceanside, I went to the restaurant where she worked and I was well liked by the employees there. This might be because I played sports and a lot of people knew my name in the Oceanside area. Delia worked at this restaurant in Oceanside for almost three years, and before I went into the military, no one who worked at the restaurant could tell her that we should not be seen together. Sure, in Oceanside, there were people who did not like seeing Delia and I together, but no one could stop her from being with me, including her father. Now that I think about it, this experience with Delia's job in Tacoma was the first time we actually experienced these kinds of problems, outside of her father. However, it was me who thought the environment in Tacoma would be good for Delia and me, but it turned out that it was that environment that helped cause our separation. I now believe I should have been stronger and refused to let her job situation be this way, even if she was fired because of our relationship. For whatever reasons, I guess it was not meant for Delia and me to stay together. When I had just about over a year left of my enlistment, Delia and I separated, just before she turned twenty-one. Even though it did not work out between Delia and me, I will never forget her or the love and the great times we spent together. I now realize her love was the greatest love that I have ever known, that I will always wish her well, and hope that she will forgive me for the hurt that I caused her. Most importantly, from this experience I vowed that I would never let my race cause me to lose anything again without a fight from me.[5]

Because I had a little over eighteen months left of my enlistment, I started talking to older African American service men about their experiences in the military. This was mainly because before entering the Army, I heard many older African Americans in Oceanside say that the military was not for an African American man. They said that the African American service member was just the "white man's boy," because African Americans can fight and die for this country, but the white society will never accept them as an equal. They said the military was just as racist as white society. I wanted to hear from the African American service members to see if they also believed that the military was just as racist as the white society, so I would ask them about their home environments before coming into the Army and their lives while in the Army. What I learned from those conversations with older African American service members was that almost all of them believed that they had many more opportunities in the military, such as a better living for their family and better chances of getting promotions than in the civilian world.

At the age of twenty-three, I had no evidence to dispute the fact that many African Americans I saw and met were doing very well in the military, and it did appear that there were opportunities for advancement in the military. Furthermore, I must say that my time in the military was not that bad because my job assignment

---

[5]   The term "fight" means to act in a non-violent way in standing up for what is mine in these kinds of situations.

was logistics, not combat. Since my job in the military was mostly working in an office setting, I had a lot of time to read magazines like Jet and Ebony. From these magazines, I read articles about many great African Americans that I did not know about because they were not talked about in my high school classes. Some of these African American leaders I do remember from my Black Study classes at Mira Costa Jr. College, but I did not have the hunger then to know more about them. What I got out of reading these articles was that the majority talked about education as a way for African Americans to get ahead in this society. I decided that I wanted to go back to school and earn an associate's degree. In 1978, I enrolled at a Jr. College at Fort Lewis determined to get an associate's degree, which I did before leaving the military in 1979. I believe that lack of education was a big factor in keeping many African Americans from gainful employment and employment opportunities.

I believed that once I had this degree, I had prepared myself for gainful employment, and if I decided not to leave the military, I could use this degree to further myself in the military.

Chapter Six

My Years with Cheryl

When I arrived at Fort Lewis in 1977, I was assigned to the 525th Welcoming Unit—these are the barracks to which every soldier is assigned when first reporting to Fort Lewis before being assigned to a permanent unit. The 525th barrack is a staging unit until the soldier's paperwork is processed. While there, I saw that Fort Lewis had two sides: one side of the fort for the infantry soldiers and the other side for the logistical units. Most of the barracks on the logistical side were co-ed, similar to what I experienced during my military schooling. Based on the military job assignment I selected before entering the Army (a Transportation Specialist), my military schooling after basic training prepared me to complete military and civilian forms to move any military vehicle by any mode of transportation.

Since my job assignment was logistical, I was assigned to the 593rd Transportation Support Group, which was on the logistical side of the fort. The 593rd Transportation Support Group had many transportation companies assigned to the group, and I was assigned to the headquarter unit. On my first day in the 593rd company barracks, I had to complete all of my administrative paperwork, and afterwards I was assigned to a room in the barracks. This was before I moved Delia to Tacoma. The barracks had three floors and a basement. The first floor was where the company commander's office and the company administrative offices were located. The second floor was where the male soldiers had their rooms, and the third floor was where the female soldiers had theirs.

The first time I saw Cheryl (who is white); I was on my way to my room in the barracks. I noticed her coming down from the third floor where the women's rooms were. She was a fine looking young woman. I thought her army fatigues looked nice on her. As we walked past each other, I had to say hello just to let her know

I noticed her. Cheryl smiled and said hello back to me as she kept walking down the stairs. When I got to my room, I saw that it was small but clean with two wall closets. Later that day I met my roommate, James. James was black and twenty-two years old and had been in the Army for a couple of years. I was twenty-three then, so James and I got along. James worked in the supply room located in the basement of the barracks. The next day, I was told to report to the 593rd Headquarter Support Group Building. This is where the top ranking officers (Colonels, Majors, and Captains) of the support group offices were located. The building also had several of the top ranking non-commissioned officers (Sergeant Majors and Master Sergeants). Additionally, women were working in many of the offices there.

When I reported to work at my assigned office, I was surprised to discover that Cheryl and I were going to be working in the same office. Cheryl and I worked in the transportation section of the Support Group. She did mainly clerical duties as well as being the driver for our section Colonel. My duties were mainly logistical support for the Ranger Company and other Infantry Companies. Our section was on a twenty-four hour alert schedule because when the Rangers or one of the Infantry Companies were doing war games we had to weigh all of the tactical vehicles they needed. They would drive their vehicles to one of the weigh stations on Fort Lewis Base where we would weigh the vehicles, then find the center of gravity of each vehicle, and mark that point for the loadmasters at McCord Air Force Base. This was critical for the loading of the cargo planes so that the planes would be balanced during their flight to the designated unloading point, in case of actual war. Our section had this drill two to three times a month, which started about 3:00 a.m. and lasted until 10:00 a.m. The rest of the time we had clean up duties around the headquarters and company barracks. Less frequently, we took turns driving the officers assigned to headquarter to the different companies within the 593rd Support Group for meetings and inspections of certain companies. When there was nothing to do we stayed around our section, but I was allowed to go to the gym often. This was mostly my daily routine.

In time, Cheryl and I became good friends. I guess it was fate, since we worked together. Cheryl did not live in the barracks for long. She and one of her friends, who was in the Army, rented an apartment in Tacoma together. I found out later from her that her roommate went to the same high school as I did, but she was younger. Her name was Mary Ann, and she recognized my name from my years of playing sports in Oceanside after Cheryl told her about me. Cheryl and I worked together during my football season at Fort Lewis, but she was always too busy with her friends to come to any of my games, and I was still married to Delia then. However, after most of the games, we would talk at work because she would read about what I did in the game from the *Ranger Newspaper*, the local military paper. Cheryl and I worked together for about eight months before she was transferred to another unit within the 593rd Transportation Support Group. While she was in this other unit, I saw her and Mary Ann every now and then. However, when she had less than a year left before it was time for her to be discharged from the Army, she used her influence with some of the top officers within the 593rd headquarter unit to be transferred back to the unit. A Colonel requested that she come back to the 593rd Headquarter Support Group building to be his secretary.

As luck would have it, she was right down the hall from where we used to work. By then Delia and I had separated, and Delia went back to California. Cheryl and I would see each other often as I was coming and going from my office. I also played racquetball regularly with the Colonel for whom she was assigned as his secretary, and so I would talk to her after I visited with the Colonel pertaining to our next racquetball workout. Cheryl and I became closer when I started showing her and Mary Ann how to play racquetball at the base gym. She would invite me over to their apartment to sit around, talk, and watch T.V. They also invited me to some of their friends' house parties. Sometime in 1978, Cheryl's enlistment would have been finished. However, she heard that our unit was going to Europe for eight weeks. She was told if she re-enlisted for three more months she could also go to Europe, and when she got back, if she still wanted to, she could still be discharged from the military.

Our unit was ordered to participate in war games in Europe because we would be one of the units from the U.S. that would give logistical support to NATO (North Atlantic Treaty Organization) forces in case there was another war in Europe. We arrived in Europe in October 1978 at the start of winter and near the end of Oktoberfest in Germany, the big beer drinking festival that lasts for weeks. Cheryl and I were not together the whole time because once we got to Frankfurt the unit was divided up. Half of us went to Antwerp, Belgium and the other half went to Rotterdam, Holland. She went to Holland, and I went to Belgium.

My group traveled to Antwerp by buses made by Mercedes-Benz. These buses made Greyhound buses look obsolete because they were built like a Mercedes-Benz car, "plush." While we were traveling from Frankfurt to Antwerp, we traveled on the autobahn and got to see major cities like Heidelberg and Hamburg. When we arrived in Antwerp, we were assigned to stay at a Belgium

Army military station, which was a couple of miles outside the city of Antwerp. Our unit's mission was to support the NATO unit in moving military vehicles, such as tanks and trucks from the United States, in case war broke out in Europe. These vehicles would come from the U.S. on military cargo ships that would arrive at the Port of Antwerp. My workday consisted of looking up make believe cargo inventories and manifests which would be used during a wartime situation.

When we were done working each day, we got to wander around Antwerp. The people mainly spoke Flemish or German, so we had our escort interpret for us. After we were in Antwerp for about three or four weeks, it was time for us to leave and meet up with the other half of the company. Then the whole unit was going to a staging area in Northwest Germany not far from the port in Bremerhaven, Germany. Before leaving Antwerp, I asked my lieutenant if I could go to Rotterdam where the other half of the unit was so I could see Cheryl. My lieutenant gave me permission to my surprise, so I went back to the barracks to clean up and to get a change of clothes. After I was done, another lieutenant took me to the railroad station to make sure that I bought the right ticket and he told me if I had any problems on the trip to show my military I.D. card.

It was Friday morning when I got on the train and began my adventure to see Cheryl in Rotterdam. The train ride was interesting because I was traveling to a different country, and everything was new and exciting. I can remember seeing the countryside farms in Holland where I saw great big pigs and horses, nothing like I had ever seen in the U.S. Maybe this was because I was not raised on a farm, but they seemed so different. I remember the train going through Amsterdam and looking at the people walking around the city, wishing that I could stop at one of those smoking cafés that I had heard about back in the days when I was running the streets.

Once I got to Rotterdam, I needed to catch a bus to the Dutch Air Force Base where Cheryl and the other half of my unit were stationed. I got off the train and asked someone how to get to the bus station. I was surprised that no one coming off the train spoke English. I started to get worried, but then I saw a couple of black men walking towards my direction. I thought to myself that these U.S. brothers would surely help me out, so I approached them and asked them if they knew where the bus station was. They looked at me as if I was a foreigner and started to talk to each other in some language that I had never heard. I really began to get worried. Then out of nowhere, this older Dutch man came up to me and asked, "Are you an American?" I told him I was. He then motioned me to come with him. He took me to the Dutch Police Station where there was an English-speaking officer. After talking to me, he got on the phone and called the Dutch Air Force Base in Rotterdam. He then gave me the phone, and on the other end of the phone was Cheryl. I told her that I was at the train station in Rotterdam trying to come to see her. She was shocked and surprised because she did not know that I was coming. She found out which bus I needed to take to get to the Air Force Base.

Once I got to the base, my friend Morris was waiting for me at the spot where she had told me to go. He said that Cheryl told him that I was coming and to meet me there. He was laughing because he could not believe that I was able to come to Holland just to see her. Morris then took me to the office where she was working, and after we greeted each other, I told her that I would be with Morris until she got off. It was Friday afternoon, and once she got off work, Cheryl and I left the base believing if we stayed on the base, someone would try to stop us from being with each other. We stayed Friday and Saturday night in Rotterdam, and when Sunday mid-morning came, we went back to the Air Force Base.

When we got back, we saw Morris. He said that Sergeant Major Page was looking for me and that he drove in from Antwerp to find me. I was not worried because my assigned lieutenant had given me permission to leave and another lieutenant took me to the train station. Most of all, we knew that the Commanding Colonel said that during our time off we could go sightseeing, so I had the weekend off and I did just that. However, after hearing about Seargent Major Page, Cheryl and I both looked at each other and said, "I bet somebody got mad because we were together." We both went looking for Sergeant Major Page.

Sergeant Major Page looked a lot like "Mr. Clean," but he was black. When he saw Cheryl and me, he pulled us into an office and started in on me about me being AWOL and that I was in a whole bunch of trouble. I told him that my lieutenant had approved my leave, that another lieutenant took me to the train station, and about the statement made by the Commanding Colonel. After all that, he had nothing more to say to me. He then looked at Cheryl and said that the Headquarter Company Colonel and other high-ranking officers had been talking about her and me being together. Cheryl told him if her father could not tell her whom she could be with, then no one—not even the Colonel or anyone else—could tell her with whom she could be. Sergeant Major Page had no more to say to either one of us and nothing else was said or done to me. However, my ride back in a military vehicle to Antwerp with Sergeant Major Page and the Company Chaplin was a long silent ride. I believe if the Chaplin had not been with us, then Sergeant Major Page would have had more to say to me. Cheryl and I both knew that there were individuals, both black and white, who did not like seeing us together since the unit was supposed to be in a combat situation, but no one could make us feel like we should not be together and that we could not have fun together in this situation.

A week later, the whole company came together, and we all went to Northwest Germany to a military staging area outside of Bremerhaven. Now this area was nothing like being in the cities of Rotterdam or Antwerp. We were out in the countryside right in the middle of a big forest. We were a couple of miles away from where NATO was carrying out war game exercises. We really did not have much to do with this because it mainly involved combat personnel, and we were there only for logistical support. To me the only good part of being there for two weeks was that some of us were able to go to Luxembourg, which was not too far from where we were. I went because I was told that we were going to the area where the Battle of the Bulge took place and we were going to where General George S. Patton was buried. For some reason Cheryl did not go with me.

Before entering the military, I had seen the movie "Battle of the Bulge" many times, and it talks about Patton throughout the movie. I also knew about a side of Patton that the movie did not mention. From watching war documentaries on T.V. and from articles that I read, I knew how Patton respected and treated the black service members assigned to him. At a time when there was still a lot of racism in the military, Patton was above most of it. I read an article that said when Patton was stationed at Fort Riley, Kansas; a mob of whites from Junction City's honky-tonk row captured and threatened to kill one of Patton's black non-commissioned officers. When Patton heard of this, he ordered his cavalry to mount, borrowed a cannon and moved against this notoriously bad area. Patton threatened to level the area unless this black non-commissioned officer was released. He was promptly released. I also knew that he gave credit to his black transportation company—the Red Ball Express—that supplied his tanks with fuel during the war. So to me, I wanted to honor and pay my respects to General George S. Patton by going to his grave site in Hamm, Luxembourg and going to Bastogne to visit the war memorial there honoring the soldiers who died at the Battle of the Bulge.

When Cheryl's enlistment was completed, I still had less than a year before my enlistment was done. She decided that she would stay in the Tacoma area and go to school for an associate's degree in registered nursing. We moved in together around the first part of 1979, right before she enrolled in school. In my last year at Fort Lewis, I started working in the military household goods section of the 525th unit building. This section is where military service members would come to arrange for delivery of their personal goods. The household goods section kept track of the military personnel goods coming into Fort Lewis from different civilian moving and storage companies, which had military contracts to do this. This section also handled household goods leaving Fort Lewis and McCord Air Force Base going to different military bases around the world. I worked in the section dealing with household goods coming into Fort Lewis and McCord Air Base, and I communicated with the local civilian moving and storage companies that had contracts with the military for the storage and delivery of military household goods in the Puget Sound area. I had to set up appointments for the delivery of the household goods to the military personnel homes, and I would try to smooth out, or solve any problems with the military personnel and the moving company pertaining to any claims of damages.

During my last year in the Army, and my first year after leaving the Army, I played football for the Pierce County Bengals, which is a semi-pro football team that I played against while I was in the Army.[6] While I played for the Bengals, Cheryl was able to see my football skills because she went to most of my games to watch me play. I was glad that I had the opportunity to show her that I was as good as I told her I was, since she never had a chance to see me play when I was on the Fort Lewis team.

---

[6]   Pierce County is a county in the State of Washington and Tacoma is a city within Pierce County.

Chapter Seven

My Experience with Racial Discrimination at WCG

I needed to tell the reader about my life in the previous chapters so that the reader could understand that during this time, I was always treated as an equal to the whites with whom I came in contact, or competed against on the football field. Therefore, it was and still is against everything I know for me to be treated anything less than equal to anyone. The only exception, before West Coast Grocery (WCG) where my race was an issue, was what Delia and I experienced when she was working at that restaurant in Tacoma. Apart from that experience, I only knew that a person was measured by their worth and not by their race. However, my experience with WCG and the Ninth Circuit Court of Appeals showed me that my race is all that matters when it comes to equality for employment opportunities at WCG, and equality in applying the law relating to racial employment discrimination by the Ninth Circuit Court of Appeals. The following is my experience with the denial of employment opportunities based on race at WCG, the intentional fabrications by a Ninth Circuit Court of Appeals panel to reverse a ruling in my favor, and lastly, the unwillingness of both the entire Ninth Circuit Court of Appeals and the U.S. Supreme Court to correct the above intentional miscarriage of justice.

In **November 1979**, I left the military to find a decent paying job in the Tacoma area since Cheryl was still going to school. I knew I had ninety days to find a job paying somewhere near the pay that I was earning in the Army. If not, I would re-enlist back into the Army. I learned about WCG from one of the black running backs on the Bengals, Nate Bradford. He told me about openings at WCG and that he had just been hired in November of '79. He said that I could list him as a reference. I also talked to one of the owners of the Bengals about using him as a reference, and he said that I could for a position at WCG. He told me that he knew a corporate person at WCG, and he said he would talk to him about hiring me. I guess it was my destiny, or my ill fate, to work at WCG because on **January 15, 1980**, the last day of my ninety days to return to the Army, I was hired as a casual/part-time order selector.

I was excited to be given this opportunity even though I had been told about the discrimination in the work environment at the WCG warehouses. My friend Nate told me before I applied that WCG was hiring minorities because they needed to fulfill their non-discriminatory clause requirements so that they could keep their federal contracts. So in 1980, WCG opened its doors to minorities for equal employment opportunities in its Tacoma grocery and produce warehouses.

On **January 16, 1980**, I reported to work at the start of the graveyard shift, along with a white looking person by the name of Joe Gallagher. On the first night, we were told that we would have to go through an eight-week training period where new hires would have to meet a weekly percentage rate. This rate was how long WCG determined it should take an order selector to complete an order. Both of us completed the eight-week training period and were hired as part-time order selectors. We then had to join the Teamster's Union, but had no union protection until WCG hired us as full-time selectors. Sometime late in **1981**, after about a year or more working as casual/part-time order selectors, we both were hired full-time with all of the union and company benefits. In addition, about this time, I bought my house in the Spanaway area using my military housing benefit, and later Cheryl and I had our wedding ceremony in this house.

Before Cheryl and I were married, my sister Phyllis and Cheryl got to know each other. Phyllis and her son C.T. would drive up from Vancouver, WA (Clarence and her bought a new house in

Vancouver, which was just across the river from Portland on the Washington side) in either her Porsche or her Corvette. She was doing pretty well as a U.P.S. driver and Clarence was doing well as the first black Safeway store manager in the Portland area. During the holidays, most of the time, Cheryl and I would go to my sister's house to have dinner and interact with Clarence's family, which I knew from when Clarence and I were in high school together. This was before Cheryl and I had our first son and after Clarence and Phyllis had their second son, Joshua. Additionally, during this time that I first brought my house, my cousin Lee was assign to Fort Lewis, where he and some of his military friends would come over and hang out, or help me around the outside with the landscaping and preparing the ground for grass. These were happy times for all of us.

Sometime in **1982**, I decided to attend Fort Steilacoom Community College to earn an associate's degree in business management, thinking this degree would help with future employment opportunities at WCG. I thought this would help because Joe was now being trained in the scheduling office to become a supervisor. When I asked him how he received this advancement opportunity, he said that he thought it was because he had some college classes in the past and his family owns a grocery store. I believe Joe did not have an associate's or bachelor's degree during this time, nor did he have any of the military experience I had. Therefore, I said to myself, "I have been working here just as long as he has. I gained an associate's degree from Fort Steilacoom Community College while in the Army and because of my military experience working as a Transportation Specialist and working in the household goods section at Fort Lewis, I am as qualified as he is to be trained in the scheduling office."

Joe was hired as a supervisor in early **1983**. That same year I decided that I was going to ask for this training so that I could gain some experience for the next warehouse supervisor position opening. From what I saw, the training had very little to do with the supervising of order selectors. It seemed that it had more to do with keeping track of loading, unloading, and the staging of trailers that came to the warehouse. Joe was later hired as a warehouse supervisor after receiving this scheduling office training. Nevertheless, I continued to go to Fort Steilacoom Community College working towards both a business management degree and a business associate's degree. I earned both of these degrees eventually in **1985** and **1986** respectively.

In an effort to demonstrate my organizational skills to upper management, in the **summer of 1983**, I put together the first "bed race team" at WCG. The bed race was an annual event that was held in downtown Tacoma. I talked to one of the Corporate Officers at WCG about paying the $300.00 registration fee for a team of grocery warehouse order selectors to race in the "Muscular Dystrophy Fund Raising Bed Race." He said yes because it was a good community event, and it was good for WCG to be part of this community fund raising event. Because of my efforts, WCG was part of this community event for the first time. In addition, because of this event, I had the opportunity to show my leadership skills to the corporate officer, who was impressed by the jerseys I had made for the team, and by the bed that my friend Dan and I made for the race.

During this time, I was also talking to my immediate supervisor, Charles Young, about what the requirements were for one to receive the on-the-job-training in the scheduling office, which prepares a person for a warehouse supervisor position. During one of our many conversations, he said to me that I would have to prove to him that, "I could get along with the white order selectors" who I would be supervising. I was shocked to hear this from another black man, who was a supervisor, so I asked him how long he had been an order selector before he became a supervisor. He replied that he was never an order selector and that he was hired from California as a supervisor. Afterwards, I asked him if he had required that the white order selectors prove themselves that they could get along with the black order selectors before they received this higher paying on-the-job-training. He said no. Then I asked him if he had ever been in the military. He said no. I told him about the bed race team that I put together and organized, and that I was the only black on the team. He did not know about this. I told him that I had been with this company for over two years and that I never had any complaints from any of the white order selectors about to me not being able to get along with them.

I then asked him for the training in the scheduling office, and he said that he would think about it. I ended my conversation with him and went back to work. After our conversation, I said to myself, "This cannot be right. Why do black employees have to prove that they can get along with white employees, while white employees do not have to prove that they can get along with black employees? And why should this be a prerequisite for receiving training?" In addition, I realized that "Charles had just told me that a black person could get into supervision without being an order selector." Near the **end of 1983**, three grocery warehouse supervisor positions opened, and I applied but was not selected. I believe it was because I did not have the scheduling office training like the white applicants. My suspicion was confirmed when I was told that the reason I was not considered was that I did not have the training. WCG hired three white order selectors in the early part of **1984** who had received the on-the-job-training in the scheduling office. I thought to myself, "This is totally unfair and discriminatory since only white order selectors are allowed to receive this training." I also thought back to my situation related to Delia's job here in Tacoma, where I vowed to myself that I would never let my race lose anything without a fight. Now WCG is going to see a side of me that they did not know about.

Since I worked with these three white order selectors in the warehouse, I got to know them. I knew that one of them only had a high school education, and the other two had bachelor's degrees, (the father of one was the corporate manager for WCG). In my mind, I was more qualified than the one with only the high school education, especially when taking into consideration my three years of military service and my associate degrees. When you take away the on-the-job training the three of them received, on paper I believe I was as qualified as the two white order selectors with the bachelor's degrees.

Again, I talked to Charles and he said that I could observe the training that the white order selectors had been receiving with pay, but I had to come in nights when I got off from work at 10:30 p.m. and without pay. For four nights, I stayed after work and observed what the white order selectors were being trained and taught in the scheduling office.

Later, Charles came back to me and asked me what I thought about the training that I observed. I replied that after observing the on-the-job-training that the white order selectors were receiving and being paid more than an order selector, I concluded that a "moron could be taught this job because the job duties were so easy to learn." I told him that I learned much more serious responsibilities while I was in the Army. I told him that I thought WCG was keeping this training from the black order selectors so that I and other blacks would always remain order selectors or forklift drivers. Lastly, I told Charles that order selecting was not a requirement for the supervisor position anyway because as he told me, he was never an order selector. After this, I talked to the Teamsters Union about the unwritten policy and the unequal treatment relating to this higher paying on-the-job-training that is only being offered to the white union members at WCG.

The Union really did not want to get involved until I started saying I believed it was racial discrimination. After the three white order selectors were hired as supervisors, the union asked for a meeting with the WCG Corporate Officer to discuss this matter of on-the-job-training. The Corporate Officer who represented WCG at this meeting son received this on-the-job-training and was one of the three white order selectors who were chosen to become a supervisor. After the union had its say on this matter to the WCG Corporate Officer, I wanted to make sure that the WCG Corporate Officer knew that I was asking the question. Therefore, I asked him directly, "What exactly are the requirements to receive this on-the-job-training in the scheduling office?" I told him what Charles had said to me about how I had to prove to him that I could get along with the white order selectors, but they did not have to prove that they could get along with the black order selectors. I also made it clear that I wanted the same opportunities as the white order selectors for advancement. The officer said to me, knowing that I was asking for the same opportunities that his son received, **"WCG does not like to put carrots in front of their mules; they expect their mules to do their best."** This was totally disrespectful and degrading because I believe he viewed me as property, as this corporate mule. It reminded me of the Dred Scott case that I learned about in my Black History classes at Mira Costa Jr. College where the U.S. Supreme Court viewed blacks as property. So I just smiled, got up, and left the meeting. Everybody else just sat there surprised that I was simply walking out of the meeting.

Chapter Eight

Filing My First Complaint

A couple of days after the meeting with the corporate manager and Union representatives, I went to the Tacoma branch of the National Association for the Advancement of Colored People (N.A.A.C.P). I wanted to talk to someone about what was happening at WCG surrounding this unequal employment opportunity treatment. I thought of the N.A.A.C.P. because my mother was deeply involved with them in Oceanside prior to her death and because I gave donations to them each year that, I worked at WCG during the WCG annual charity drive. However, each time I went to the Tacoma branch of the N.A.A.C.P. no one was in the office. There was a sign that said to leave a phone number with a brief message and that they would call you back. Each time I went to the branch and left messages with my phone number, no one from the branch called back. Therefore, after many attempts, I went to the Seattle branch of the N.A.A.C.P.

There, at least, I got to talk to the President of the branch, Oscar Eason. He said because I did not live in the Seattle area, and because WCG was not in the Seattle area, his branch could not help me. A few days later, I contacted the local branch of the Urban League in Tacoma to tell them about what I believed to be racial discrimination at WCG. The lady who worked at the Urban League told me that I needed to talk to Aaron Lee and that he worked at the Tacoma Human Rights Office. She said this because Mr. Lee was known in the black community, in Tacoma, as a person who fairly investigates racial discrimination under the Federal Department of Housing and Urban Development (HUD). In addition, the department he worked for investigated employment discrimination complaints under a certification by the Equal Employment Opportunities Commission (EEOC).

I then went home and called the Tacoma Human Rights Office to talk to Aaron Lee. Mr. Lee was in the office when I called, and he set up an appointment for me to come in and talk to him. I believe this was sometime near **April of 1984**, because Cheryl's and my first son Elijah was only a baby, and close to being one year old. During my meeting with Mr. Lee, I told him about what I believed was racial discrimination at WCG. I also told him about my efforts to get the N.A.A.C.P. involved. He believed that I might have a case of racial employment discrimination based on what I had told him. Mr. Lee told me that he believed that I met my *"prima facie"* burden. According to Barrow's Law Dictionary prima facie means,

One in which the evidence is sufficient to support but not to compel a certain conclusion and does no more than furnish evidence to be considered and weighed but not necessarily to be accepted by the trier of the fact.

Mr. Lee showed me that according to EEOC and the U.S. Supreme Court, I could file a complaint under Title VII of the 1964 Civil Rights Act (42 U.S.C. 2000e) against WCG. Then he showed me that the employee must establish a *prima facie* case of racial employment discrimination, where the employee must show that:

1) The individual belongs to a racial minority;
2) The individual applied and was qualified for a job (or training) for which the employer was seeking applicants;
3) Despite the individual's qualifications, they were rejected; and

4) After the rejection, the position (or training) remained open
and the employer continued to seek applicants from persons
of the complainants' qualifications.[7]

Mr. Lee said, "according to EEOC guidelines and U.S. Supreme
Court case law, if WCG is allowing the white employees to be
trained for promotional opportunity, then the black employees must
be provided this same opportunity".

Since WCG had this on-the-job-training for which I believed
I was qualified; since I was black and was rejected; since WCG
continued to offer this training to other white order selectors, I
believed I met my prima facie case burden according to EEOC
guidelines and federal law. Mr. Lee suggested that I should file a
complaint with the EEOC, or with the Washington State Human
Rights Commission (WSHRC). Mr. Lee said that the WSHRC
has a federal contract with EEOC to do investigations according
to EEOC guidelines, when individuals file a complaint with them
under Title VII of the 1964 Civil Rights Act. He also said that in
the past, WCG had blocked him from doing investigations when
other WCG employees had filed complaints against WCG with
him at the Tacoma Human Rights Office. Based on Mr. Lee's past
experience with WCG pertaining to allegations of racial employment
discrimination, he encouraged me to file with the EEOC or the
WSHRC soon because there is only a certain amount of time to file
with one of these agencies. So sometime in **July 1984,** I filed my
first compliant against WCG with the WSHRC (**).[8] Prior to filing

---

[7]   *McDonnell Douglas Corp. v. Green*, 411 U.S. 792 (1973).

[8]   (**)means document can be located at the U.S. Federal Archive
Building in Seattle, WA case#C86-528T *Stroman v. West Coast
Grocery* shipment #5125, accession #21920003, box #24, and the
location #33005.

my complaint with the WSHRC, I asked Mr. Lee if he would teach me what I needed to know about Title VII to prove a complaint of racial employment discrimination. He said, "Of all my previous complainants, no one has ever asked me to teach them how to prove a case of racial employment discrimination." He said that he would teach me what the EEOC requires and what federal case law states is needed to prove a case of individual racial employment discrimination in federal court. So after work, and in between my school time, I would go to Mr. Lee's house where he told me about the history of the 1964 Civil Rights Act. He said that the Act was landmark legislation because it prohibits discrimination by covered employers (employers with fifteen or more employees).

Title VII under the 1964 Civil Rights Act was first conceived to help African Americans, but later was expanded to include sex and age discrimination. Mr. Lee also told me that along with this Act, Congress established EEOC to investigate complaints of employment discrimination and complaints of retaliation for filing a complaint under this Act. I learned that EEOC has the power to issue *right to sue letters* if EEOC, or one of their contract agencies, cannot settle the dispute between an employee and a covered employer. In addition, after EEOC finishes its investigation and issues a ruling, the employee receives a *right to sue letter.* Then once the EEOC issues a *right to sue letter,* the employee has only ninety days to file a complaint, (a lawsuit) in federal district court against the employer to let a federal court judge decide the issue(s). With the *right to sue letter,* an employee can file a lawsuit regardless if EEOC rules in favor of the employee or the employer.

Mr. Lee gave me EEOC manuals to read that explain how to investigate employment discrimination and how to interpret federal case laws on racial employment discrimination, so that I could gain knowledge about what I needed for my case to prove my allegations of discrimination. However, after reading many of the cases in the manuals I told Mr. Lee I had not read one case where the plaintiff in a racial employment discrimination case won in federal court. All I read is how the employer rebutted the plaintiff's prima facie case. Mr. Lee stated, "That is what you need to know, and I will show you from these manuals about comparative evidence and direct evidence to show pretext so WCG won't be able to rebut your prima facie case." For example, comparative evidence in my case is when a black employee claims that white employees are consistently being treated more favorably than black employees with regard to on-the-job training for promotional opportunities. This kind of evidence is probative (which means to persuade one as to the truth of an allegation) of different treatment of similarly situated employees (those in the same job category) of different races. Direct evidence is the unwritten policies that WCG uses to subjectively choose who it wants to train in the schedule office. Both of these evidences can show pretext, which means WCG's stated reasons for not allowing me the training were excuses to hide their real intentions.

After I learned what comparative and direct evidence were from the EEOC manuals on how to investigate allegations of racial employment discrimination, I knew that based upon Charles Young's statement to me that he had never been an order selector I would be able to show that order selecting is not a requirement to become a supervisor. Further evidence of this fact was a white female who worked in the personnel office, never was an order selector though was able to receive the scheduling office training, and later was hired as a supervisor after I was denied the training. I knew I could show from comparative evidence, and direct evidence that order selecting is not a requirement to receive the training in the scheduling office. Based on these two examples I knew I could show that order selecting was not a requirement to be trained or to become a supervisor. Furthermore, since WCG had no written policies on the requirements to receive the scheduling office training for all warehouse employees, I knew I could show from direct evidence that only white employees were being chosen to receive the scheduling office training. Based on the above I believed that I could show that WCG's reasons for not allowing me the scheduling office training were *pretext*.

Mr. Lee also told me about Executive Order 11246, since I told him that WCG has a federal contract to supply groceries to the military commissaries in Washington and Alaska. Under Executive Order 11246, an employer agrees not to discriminate in the workplace as long as the employer is doing business with the federal government. This meant that WCG had an obligation not to discriminate both under this Executive Order and under Title VII of the 1964 Civil Rights Act.

A couple of months after I filed my complaint with the WSHRC, they ordered a fact-finding conference relating to my complaint. A fact-finding conference is held after the WSHRC has accepted a complaint and notified the employer by issuing a formal complaint to them. So in my case the fact-finding conference was held to see if I had met my *prima facie* case and if I had any supporting evidence and/or witnesses. Additionally, the conference was held to find out WCG's non-discriminatory reasons for it's defense to the allegations of racial employment discrimination relating to my denial of receiving the scheduling office training, and to allow me to show that WCG's non-discriminatory reasons are not true (pretext).

Lastly, another purpose of the conference was to see if both WCG and I could come to an agreement to settle my complaint.

Beverly Johnson (acting as my attorney) and I attended the fact-finding conference as well as WCG's agent that was requested by the investigator for the WSHRC. During the meeting, I said to both the WSHRC and WCG agents that all I was asking for, at this level, was the same higher pay on-the-job-training in the scheduling office as the white order selectors were receiving. WCG's agents stated that I was not given the training because I was not a satisfactory employee. They also stated that the warehouse supervisors pick who they want to receive the training, that there was no written policy pertaining to the qualifications for the training in the scheduling office, and no black order selector had been selected for the training. I stated to the WSHRC that I never received any written reprimand or suspension according to the Union and WCG contract saying that I was not performing my job duties in a satisfactory manner. Additionally, WCG has no evidence to show that according to the Union contract that I was given any written reprimand or suspension for unsatisfactory job performance (this is direct evidence).

My comparative evidence included Charles, the white female personnel officer, and a white order selector (who had a suspension and a written reprimand in his file, but still was allowed to receive the paid, on-the-job training in the scheduling office).

Beverly Johnson also tried to get WCG agents to settle my complaint with the on-the-job-training issue. She said during the meeting that WCG agents did not articulate any legal or business reasons why I was not given the same opportunity as the white order selectors for this training in the scheduling office. She told them, "If Mr. Stroman hired me; I would file a complaint in federal district court on his behalf." WCG agents and their attorneys refused to give me the training in the scheduling office, and the WSHRC did nothing further regarding my complaint that I had filed with them.

After I filed my first complaint with the WSHRC, another black co-worker, Don Gluade and I asked Charles for the training in the scheduling office. Don had been working as an order selector for many years before I was hired as an order selector. Charles told Don he could not receive this training because his size would intimidate the white order selectors, and because he believed that I was militant. Because I stood up for my rights, he was not going to let me receive the training. Don looked surprised by what Charles had said to him, and I told Charles he was crazy. I told Charles if "militant" means standing up for one's right to be treated equally in a non-violent way, then I was a militant. To me it seemed that Charles, being a black man had forgotten that many blacks have fought, suffered, and died for the right to be treated as equal to any other man in this country. I later reported what Charles said to Don and me to the WSHRC, but the WSHRC never interviewed Don or investigated my complaint during the year and half that the agency had my first complaint.

Sometime in the early part of **1985**, WCG hired a different operations manager by the name of Dave Hamlin. The operations manager before Dave was Pete Clarke. I talked to Mr. Clarke during the previous interview process when I applied for the supervisor position, and he told me that the supervisor picks the order selectors for the training in the scheduling office. Based on Charles' actions, I went to this new operations manager. I approached this new manager in a polite way, introduced myself, and told him about my attempts to receive this on-the-job-training. After listening to me, he told me that he had a book for me to read that would help in my efforts to receive this on-the-job-training at WCG. This book was *Up from Slavery* by Booker T. Washington.

Chapter Nine

Filing My Second Complaint

I accepted this book *Up from Slavery* from Dave on a Friday afternoon before leaving from work. I was working swing shift at that time. I read that paperback book Friday night, all day Saturday, and while on my breaks at work on Sunday afternoon. While at work, some of my co-workers saw me reading this book and asked me why I was reading it. I told them that Dave gave it to me to read and that it was supposed to help me get the training in the scheduling office for which I had been asking. I also told them that I did not know how this book was going to help because most of what I read did not apply to me, or the time in which we were living. I also thought the book was degrading to me since I was born over a hundred years after slavery, and was born and raised in liberal California. While living in California I learned that individuals were judged by one's merits and not by some philosophy pertaining to slavery over a hundred years ago.

Monday afternoon, I went to Dave's office to give this book back to him. When he reached out to accept the book from me, I asked him, "What exactly was I supposed to get out of this book?" He said that he had not read the book and that he was just testing me to see how long it would take me to read it, because he used to be a teacher. After Dave said this, I thought to myself, reading this book is another example showing how I had to do something that the white order selectors did not have to do. I realized this book was not intended to help me in my efforts to receive the training in the scheduling office, as Dave had said.

I said to him, "Since you have not read the book, here are four pages of quotes that I got out of the book." I told him one of the quotes from the book said, ". . . negro youth must work harder, must perform his task even better than a white youth in order to secure recognition." I told Dave "I do not believe I should have to work harder than the white order selectors in order to receive this training in the scheduling office."

Dave had nothing to say to me about this quote when I told him this; rather he stood there looking shocked. I gave Dave my list of quotes from the book, which included among other quotes, ". . . no white American ever thinks that any other race is wholly civilized until he wears the white man's clothes, eats the white man's food, speaks the white man's language and professes the white man's religion." I also told him, "I need not have to do any of the above to have the same rights and job opportunities as the white employees at WCG." Afterwards, I walked out of his office.

On **April 8, 1985**, a little time after the book incident, WCG suspended me for alleged insubordination, which was approved by Dave, because I refused to talk to a supervisor without a union representative. My refusal was because my supervisor's conversation started by asking me why I did not follow his instructions concerning an inventory count I did a week earlier. At the time, Charles had another supervisor with him, so I requested that a union representative be there with me to hear what was said. My shop steward told WCG that I had a right, according to the collective bargaining agreement to have a shop steward with me, and that the suspension was not according to the union contract. The Teamsters Union agreed that the suspension was in violation of the collective bargaining agreement and filed a complaint with the National Labor Relations Board (NLRB) on my behalf.

I believe sometime in **May 1985**, WCG wanted me to settle this dispute. Part of the settlement was that they would withdraw the suspension and pay me for my time lost but I had to waive my right to use this incident (the suspension that led to the complaint with the NLRB) against them in any future disputes between us.

When I read this agreement, I did not like what I read, and since the NLRB agent came to my house with the agreement, I had my wife Cheryl read it too. She told me not to sign it the way it was written, because someone did not want me to use this incident against WCG. The NLRB agent agreed with Cheryl that I could not use this incident against WCG if I had signed it the way WCG had it written. Therefore, I reworded the agreement and told the agent that I would accept the agreement, on the terms that I could use this suspension to file another complaint with the WSHRC, to show that WCG had retaliated against me based on my efforts to receive the training in the scheduling office. So on **June 7, 1985**, I signed an agreement with WCG stating I would settle my charge with the NLRB in exchange for the conditions in the agreement as I had worded it (**).[9]

Later I told Aaron Lee about what had been going on, and he said that now WCG was starting to retaliate against me and that I should let the WSHRC know about this. So in **June of 1985**, I filed my second complaint with the WSHRC for retaliation. According to 29 CFR (code of federal regulations) 24.104 (d)(2), and EEOC guidelines, to establish a prima facie case for retaliation, one must show that he/she:

1) Engaged in a protected activity (by filing a complaint of racial employment discrimination);
2) Was thereafter subjected to adverse employment action from the employer; and

---

[9] Located at the U.S. Federal Archive Building in Seattle, WA case #C86-528T *Stroman v. West Coast Grocery,* shipment #5125, accession #21920003, box #24, location #33005.

3) There is a causal connection between the protected activity and the adverse action.

Because I believed I met these requirements, I filed a second complaint with the WSHRC based on the following:

a) My suspension in April,
b) I was denied sick pay,
c) No white order selector had to read a book from an operation manager to receive the on-the-job-training, and
d) Those who did not oppose discriminatory practices were not treated unfairly.

This second complaint can also be found in the U.S. Federal Archive Building in Seattle, WA under case #86-528T, *Stroman v. West Coast Grocery.*

When I filed the second complaint with WSHRC, I did not have an attorney because I could not afford to hire Beverly Johnson, or anybody else, so I was on my own to fight WCG and their attorneys. Fighting against a major corporation like WCG and WCG's attorneys for me was as insurmountable a challenge as the story of David versus Goliath.

After I filed the second complaint with the WSHRC they did not request a fact-finding conference, nor did they investigate my second complaint. I now believe there were several reasons the WSHRC never investigated my complaints. First, I could not afford to hire Beverly Johnson as my attorney. Second, WCG's agent had an influence on the state agency when they tried to discredit me by claiming I was a "problem employee," though it was clear that these allegations were actually retaliation on WCG's part against me for exercising my federal rights. Third, I was exposing the discriminatory practices of WCG.

I believe in **July of 1985**, WCG announced that there was another opening for a warehouse supervisor. Again, I applied for the position, and again I was not selected. Dave, however, interviewed everybody who had applied for the position, except for me. He said that he did not need to interview me and that I was simply not qualified, which I thought was retaliatory based on the "*Up from Slavery*" book incident and the suspension incident which led to the NLRB settlement agreement between WCG and me. There was no way I was not qualified to be interviewed because by that time I had two associate degrees, had observed the operations of the schedule office, and had passed his test of reading the "Up from Slavery" book in a 'timely fashion.' In my opinion, all of that demonstrated that I was at the very least qualified for an interview.

After all that I had gone through over the past three years, I decided to take an unpaid medical leave of absence. Therefore, in **August 1985**, I went on an unpaid medical leave of absence due to the stress that I was suffering from working at WCG. While on this unpaid medical leave of absence, I told a few of my friends, "I feel like quitting and going back to California where I never experienced this kind of racial treatment."

Chapter Ten

The November 1, 1985 Document

It had been over a year and a half **(from 1984-1985)**, and none of my witnesses were interviewed by the WSRHC. The treatment at WCG towards me kept getting worse. Due to WCG's actions—discrimination, retaliation, and the denial of having an interview for a promotion based on my filing complaints with the WSHRC, I went on an unpaid medical leave for ninety days. The mental anguish over the last three years at WCG was too much for me to endure, so I sought medical help for stress, depression, not being able to sleep and eat, and not wanting to be around my wife. While on this leave, doctors treated me for the stress of working in a discriminatory workplace, for my sleeping and eating problems, and I received counseling regarding my relationship with my wife.

While on this leave of absence I told two of my friends, Rich and Dan (who still worked at WCG) that I wanted to quit WCG and go back to California.[10] Sometime in late **September 1985,** a few days before I had to report back to work from my unpaid medical leave, they each came to my home separately (on different days) to tell me about a lay-off, with unemployment benefits, that WCG was offering to all the full-time permanent order selectors. They both told me Willie Mosley made this offer in Dave's presence, to all of the full-time permanent order selectors on their shift, which was the same shift I had been working before going on the unpaid medical leave. They told me about this lay-off offer because I had told them previously that I would like to go back to California to try to find a job as a warehouse person and this lay-off with unemployment benefits could help me if I decided to look for work in California.

---

[10]   These two white individuals were among my close friends while I was employed at WCG, and they were members of the bed race team that I organized.

The unemployment benefits did not come near the amount of money that I was making as an order selector, but it was better than nothing. I was going to quit if the work environment did not improve for me; and I sincerely believed it would not improve.

Willie Mosley was a black supervisor in the chain of command at WCG who was between Dave and Charles. I said to both of my friends since I had to report back to WCG for work on swing shift that coming Sunday that I would call Willie to find out if he did indeed offer this lay off at the swing shift daily meeting. The next day, I went over to the house of another friend who used to work at WCG as an order selector with me on the graveyard shift.[11] He also knew Rich and Dan, and I told him what they had said to me about the lay-off offer by Willie Mosley. I told him that I was going to call Willie about it and that I wanted him to listen on his other phone so I would have a witness to what Willie and I discussed. I knew WCG wanted me to quit, but I wanted a witness to hear the terms surrounding why I was quitting, because I did not believe that I could collect unemployment benefits if I quit.

I called Mosley at WCG from my friend's house. When Mosley answered the phone (I did not tell him that I had David on the other phone listening), I asked him if he made this lay off offer to the order selectors. Mosley said yes, he did make this announcement, but if I accepted the offer, I would have to give up my union recall rights. Rich and Dan never said anything to me about giving up any rights. I told Mosley that I would only sign away my union recall rights in exchange for unemployment benefits so that I could look for another job in the grocery industry in California. I told Mosley over the phone that I would come into his office to sign the agreement the

---

[11]   David was a non-black friend of mine during and after his employment at WCG.

next day, which was a Friday. During the entire phone conversation my friend Dave was on the other phone listening.

On Friday, however, I decided not to go to Mosley's office to sign the agreement so that I could have the weekend to talk to other swing and graveyard shift order selectors to find out if Mosley had made the offer of a lay-off and if they had to waive their union recall rights. All of the order selectors I asked said that Mosley had made this offer of a lay-off during a shift meeting, but none of them knew anything about waiving any recall rights. On Sunday, I reported to work at my normal assigned time, so that I could talk to a shop steward, pertaining to my having to waive my union recall rights to receive the lay-off when nobody else knew anything about this. When I went to clock in, my time card was not there, so I went to the scheduling office to find out why. I talked to my supervisor, John, who told me that Willie told him that I had quit. I told John that I had not quit yet; I had just been thinking about it. He then said that I would have to talk to Willie. So, I told John to call Willie at home, because Willie did not work on Sunday. After John called Willie, he gave the phone to me and left the office. Willie said to me that he thought I would be in two days ago (on Friday) to sign this agreement and quit my position at WCG. I told him that I did not trust him so I did not come in on Friday. Willie again said that I would only be giving up my recall rights and that I could trust him, so I said O.K. I will be in tomorrow morning, which was Monday.

Monday I went to Mosley's office to sign the proposed document believing that I could trust him on what he stated to me during our two phone conversations. Mosley presented me with a document that I had never seen before, nor taken any part in drafting (**see exhibit 1**). I read it. I again said to Mosley, "I am only agreeing to waive my union recall rights"; and Mosley again said that WCG "only wanted me to waive my union recall rights."[12]

I said, "I have told you that my union recall rights are the only rights that I am willing to waive, and if you are still stating the only rights that I am waiving are my union recall rights, then I will sign this document," which I did. That night, after Mr. Lee came home from work, I took the document to Mr. Lee's house so that he could read what I had signed. As soon as he got to paragraph number six, he said that there was going to be a problem. Paragraph six states "These terms represent a full and final settlement of any and all claims arising out of Mike's employment with West Coast Grocery." Even though I never intended to waive my rights to sue WCG, he believed that WCG was going to argue that I waived my rights to sue them based on paragraph six. He then said that I should have an attorney look at this document despite Mosley's statement that the only rights I was waiving were my recall rights and not any rights to sue WCG.

The next day I went to apply for my unemployment benefits. At first, the Washington State Unemployment Security Office denied me the unemployment benefits stating that I cannot quit my job in order to receive unemployment benefits. I then called Willie at work and told him what the unemployment office had told me, and that I wanted my job back since I could not collect unemployment. The next day I was called by the unemployment office to come in, because they had talked to WCG, and they said I could now receive my unemployment benefits even though I had quit my job at WCG. This shows that WCG has a lot of influence here in the State of Washington because they can get the state

---

[12]   The document itself did not state it was a termination agreement or waiver agreement.

unemployment office to break state and federal unemployment benefits laws so that I could receive unemployment benefits. As soon as I started collecting my unemployment benefits, I realized that WCG probably used their influence to stop the WSRHC from investigating my two complaints of violations of Title VII under the 1964 Civil Rights Act.

A short time after leaving WCG on this lay off, WCG was bought by SuperValu, an even larger grocery corporation. On **December 2, 1985**, before I left to go to California to apply at grocery warehouses in the California area, I filed my third complaint with the WSHRC. (**) This retaliation complaint was for the denial of being interviewed for the last supervisor position for which I applied and for causing me to go on an unpaid medical leave of absence due to the stress from the discriminatory work environment—all of which led me to quit my job at WCG. I did this believing that the WSRHC would not investigate this complaint either, but I needed to have all violations of my Title VII rights filed with this agency in case I filed a complaint in federal court against WCG.

Before leaving for California—sometime between November and December—I also talked to an attorney, Hugh McGavick, about representing me in a suit against WCG. I told McGavick about the *November 1, 1985 document*, and he told me not to worry about it because I had evidence to show that WCG offered this lay-off to all the full time order selectors without requiring them to give up their recall rights, and I never intended to waive my rights to sue WCG. McGavick said he would represent me, and I signed a contingency fee agreement with him. I also told him about me leaving to go to California to find work. I told McGavick, "Even if I find work in California I still may want to pursue a discrimination case against WCG in federal court." Two days after Christmas, I left for California.

After three months, I could not find gainful employment in the grocery industry in California, so in **March 1986**, I came back to Tacoma, WA to try to find gainful employment and to be with my family. After returning to Tacoma, I filled out forms requesting the WSHRC to issue me a right to sue letter on all three of my complaints so that I could pursue my allegations in federal court according to Title VII. Sometime in **April,** the WSHRC issued a right to sue letter on each of the first two complaints, but did not want to issue me a right to sue letter on the third complaint.

The WSHRC investigator, Rick Ramseth, told me that the WCG attorney told him that I had waived my right to sue WCG based on an agreement letter that I signed. I told him that he was crazy, and that I never waived my rights to file my racial employment discrimination complaints against WCG in federal court. At this point, I realized that Mosley had lied to me about the *November 1, 1985 document*, and that Mr. Lee was right about paragraph number six. I asked Mr. Ramseth "Did you know that I had already received a right to sue letter for each of my first two complaints against WCG after I had already signed the *November 1, 1985 document*?" He said yes, but they should not have been sent to me because when I signed the *November 1, 1985 document* I waived all my complaints against WCG.

I then asked him if the EEOC or the WSHRC had a form where an individual would check a box stating they wanted to withdraw their complaint and state why they were withdrawing their complaint. (I already knew that both agencies had such forms based on my request for my right to sue letters on my previous two complaints with the WSHRC). He said yes. I then asked him whether I had formally withdrawn my complaints with the WSHRC through this process, or given any reasons why I was withdrawing

my complaints as instructed on the form. He again stated no.
Therefore, I stated that he had no withdrawal form on file with the
EEOC or the WSHRC where I stated, based on this *November 1,
1985 document,* that I was withdrawing my complaints. He said
no. I told him that if I were withdrawing my complaints, based on
the *November 1, 1985 document,* I would have checked the box
stating that I was withdrawing my complaints with EEOC or the
WSHRC and I would have had to state why I was withdrawing my
complaints. If I had done the above then the two right to sue letters
would not have been sent to me from the WSHRC.

I told him that I was going to write to the EEOC about the fact
the WSHRC had never investigated any of my three complaints.
Additionally, I believe my third right to sue letter was denied based
solely upon WCG attorneys' or WCG agents' statements and that
I believe this was illegal and discriminatory. I then hung up the
phone.

A few days after I had talked to Rick Ramseth, I just happened
to run into Allen J. Correll, Director of the Tacoma Human Rights
Office at a community meeting. I met him through Mr. Lee. I told
Mr. Correll about the WSHRC denying my third right to sue letter.
From a Tacoma Human Relations News article dated February
1982 that I obtained from Mr. Lee, I knew about Mr. Correll's years
working with enforcement of anti-discrimination law. The article
stated in part, ". . . Additionally, such enforcement activities must be
accomplished in a timely fashion with equity." Given my situation,
this statement particularly stood out to me. So I told Mr. Correll
that the WSHRC had my first complaint for more than one and half
years and never talked to any of my witnesses (regarding black
employees being denied training in the scheduling office at WCG
for promotional opportunities), nor ever made a determination on

that complaint. Additionally, after having my second complaint for about six months, they made no determination on my complaint of retaliation. Yet suddenly, after only four months, the WSHRC decided to make a determination on my third complaint (about being denied an interview for a supervisor position at WCG). I also told him that the investigator for my third complaint, Rick Ramseth, said that I had waived my federal rights to sue WCG based only on statements by WCG's attorneys (or agents) and that he denied my third right to sue letter, and told me that I should not have even received the other two right to sue letters. After my conversation with Mr. Correll, he said that he would talk to William Gladden, the WSHRC Director, about the denial of my third right to sue letter.

After receiving my first two right to sue letters, I went back to see Hugh McGavick. I told him that I wanted my right to sue letters filed in federal court because I had only ninety days according to EEOC guidelines, or I would lose my right to sue WCG on my allegations of racial employment discrimination under Title VII of the 1964 Civil Rights Act. I also told him about my denial of the third right to sue letter. McGavick told me not to worry because anything that happened during my employment with WCG would come out during the trial. McGavick then said that he would file the right to sue letters and a complaint in federal court in Tacoma in a few weeks.[13]

---

[13] In addition, if for some reason one cannot find an attorney to file the right to sue letter within the ninety days requirement, before the ninety days has expired under certain circumstances one may petition the federal district court under Title VII to appoint an attorney to represent the individual.

EXHIBIT #1

WEST COAST GROCERY CO.

P. O. BOX 2237 / 1525 EAST "D" ST. / TACOMA, WASHINGTON 98401 / (206) 593-3200

November 1, 1985

West Coast Grocery and Grady Michael Stroman agree to the following:

1. Mike will leave the Company on an economic lay-off.

2. West Coast will not contest the unemployment benefits.

3. The employee's record will be cleared and information given out limited to date of hire, rate of pay, and journeyman status.

4. The employee will have no recall rights.

5. The employee will be entitled to any accrued vacation and his share of Profit Sharing payable as defined by Federal Law, and the terms of the Profit Sharing Trust.

6. These terms represent a full and final settlement of any and all claims arising out of Mike's employment with West Coast Grocery.

David Hamlin
West Coast Grocery Company

Willie Mosley
West Coast Grocery Company

Grady Michael Stroman

Chapter Eleven

Filing under the 1964 Civil Rights Act in Federal Court

Sometime in **June,** I went back to McGavick's office to find out if he had filed my right to sue letters and a complaint in federal court. He said that he had not, but he would file my complaint under the 1964 Civil Rights Act in Federal District Court before the ninety days were up. Filing a complaint in federal court under the 1964 Civil Rights Act establishes that I had filed complaint(s) with the EEOC for racial discrimination under Title VII, and those rights to sue letter(s) were issued by the EEOC. The right to sue letters gave me the authority to file the EEOC complaint(s) in federal court to let a federal judge rule on the allegation(s)—in other words, a lawsuit. When a person receives his/her, right to sue letter and files a complaint in a federal court, the federal court knows that both parties know exactly why they are there—a lawsuit for intentional racial employment discrimination.

Before McGavick filed my complaint in federal court, all I knew about the federal district court in Tacoma was that there were two federal judges—Judge Jack Tanner (who was black) and Judge Robert Bryan (who was white). I heard that Judge Tanner was known as "Maximum Jack" for the long sentences he handed out to individuals who were found to be guilty, and that he once was a civil rights attorney in the Tacoma area before becoming a federal judge. I also learned that he disagreed with the federal government's attorneys when he ruled in favor of Native Americans pertaining to fishing rights in Washington State. Additionally, Aaron (Mr. Lee) told me that McGavick's father and Tanner were law partners before Tanner became a federal judge.

In **July of 1986**, McGavick filed the right to sue letters as well as a complaint in federal court in Tacoma case #C86-528T (**see exhibit 2**). When I found out that Judge Tanner would be hearing my case, I was glad, mainly because he was black. I believed he would easily see I was not given the same opportunities as the white order selectors at WCG.

At first, Mr. Lee was also happy that Judge Tanner would be hearing my case, but then he said that it would have been even better if Judge Bryan were hearing my case. He said this because he feared that, if I should win, some people would say it was only because both Judge Tanner and I are black, even though Mr. Lee had not heard of any blacks proving a case of racial employment discrimination in Judge Tanner's courtroom. Mr. Lee had enough experience with the 1964 Civil Rights Act that he knew I could win on the merits of my case no matter what race the judge was as, long as he looked at the facts according to Title VII of the1964 Civil Rights Act and the EEOC mandate. However, Mr. Lee had a feeling that race would be a factor if Judge Tanner ruled in my favor. I received the third right to sue letter from the EEOC after my complaint was filed in federal court, and I gave it to McGavick, but I do not believe he filed it in federal court because he did not amend the complaint to add the issues that were in my third complaint filed with the WSHRC. My actions showed that I never considered waiving my rights under the 1964 Civil Rights Act.

Since my wife Cheryl was a registered nurse with about three years of experience, we decided that she would financially take care of the family, and I would raise the boys while searching for employment. So while waiting to go to court, I was filling out applications for employment in California (as a correction officer) and the Tacoma area (as state patrol officer and general entry-level positions) as well as taking care of my sons. However, before getting into court, in **January of 1987**, I had to participate in a deposition, and sit in on depositions from my witnesses, Don Glaude and Ed Haskins in **March of 1987**. During my deposition, a WCG attorney, Timothy Whitters, asked me about the *November 1, 1985 document,* which I told him Mosley had tricked me into signing. I told him that the WSHRC tried to deny my third right to sue letter based on this document but later they issued the third right to sue letter. I told Mr. Whitters I never intended to waive my right to sue WCG for employment discrimination. Then I told him that when I signed the document Willie Mosley was fully aware that I only intended to waive my union recall rights, which are the only rights mentioned in the document. In addition, I told Mr. Whitters that I had a friend listen to my phone conversation with Mosley so that I would have a witness hearing me tell him that I was only waiving my union recall rights.

After the depositions, WCG attorneys knew exactly what evidence I had against them. In **May of 1987**, after the discovery phase WCG attorneys motioned the court for a summary judgment[14] **(**)**. According to Barrow's Law Dictionary,

> *Summary judgment* is a device designed to effect a prompt disposition of controversies on their merits without resort to a lengthy trial, if in essence there is no real dispute as to salient facts or if only a question of law is involved.

Their basis for a motion for summary judgment was that they felt there was no real dispute because according to them I waived my right to sue WCG by signing the *November 1, 1985 document.* Attached to their motion was an affidavit from Willie Mosley and excerpts of my deposition.

---

[14]   In a pre-trial procedure, each party in the lawsuit exchanges the other party's information and takes depositions of the other party's witnesses.

On **June 15, 1987**, my attorney, Hugh McGavick, then filed a memorandum of opposition (**see exhibit 3**) stating that, in so many words, Mosley was lying and that I had a witness to prove it (******). In McGavick's memorandum he stated, according to federal case law WCG did not prove that I knowingly, intentionally, and voluntarily waived my federal rights to sue WCG.[15] According to the U.S. Supreme Court ruling in Alexander v. Gardner-Denver Co., 415 U.S. 36, 94 S.Ct. 1011, 39 L.Ed.2d 147 (1974), the court stated,

> [A]n employee may waive his cause of action under Title VII as part of a voluntary settlement. In determining the effectiveness of any such waiver, a Court would have to determine at the outset that the employee's consent to the suit was voluntary and knowing.

McGavick also stated under contract law the *November 1, 1985 document* was unenforceable. He stated,

> In Washington State, it is clear that a contract may be either reformed or rescinded when the contract is based upon a material misrepresentation. In such instances, proof of fraud is not necessary to show misrepresentation.

Because Mosley acted intentionally in representing the effect and meaning of the sixth paragraph to me, the outcome constitutes fraud in the inducement, making the *November 1, 1985 document* unenforceable. Additionally, attached to McGavick's motion was

---

[15]   The evidence on the court record only showed that I intended to waive my union recall rights.

my affidavit dated **June 16, 1987** (**see exhibit 4**), and excerpts of my deposition where I disputed what Mosley had stated related to the *November 1, 1985 document*. (******)

While WCG and I waited for Judge Tanner's ruling on the summary judgment motion, both parties had to attend a 39.1 meeting that was ordered by the court sometime in **late June of 1987**, because my trial date was **August 10, 1987**. The purpose of a 39.1 meeting is for both parties to come together and present their side of the story to a mediator (who is also an attorney, but not representing either party). The mediator weighs the merits of both sides, and afterwards, tries to determine if there is any way that both parties can settle the case, besides going to trial.

I took Mr. Lee with me to this 39.1 meeting in case I needed his advice. During this meeting WCG's attorney, Elizabeth Martin, started off by talking about how bad an employee I was and how my white co-workers could not get along with me. Then McGavick started talking about how I would not win at the summary judgment motion. Mr. Lee stopped McGavick and said WCG submitted no evidence that I knew I was waiving my rights under the 1964 Civil Rights Act. The mediator saw that I was smiling and asked me why I was smiling. I said,

> McGavick knows that I never intended to waive my rights not to go to court pertaining to my allegations of racial employment discrimination and retaliation against WCG. However, I admitted that I was not the best order selector at WCG, but I had comparative evidence to show that one did not need to be a good order selector or an order selector at all, in order to receive the scheduling office training or be a warehouse supervisor.

Also, I said,

> If I was such a bad employee at WCG, here is their
> chance to show that I was by having written warnings
> or reprimands stating that I was not performing my
> job functions in a satisfactory matter according to the
> collective bargaining agreement.

I worked at WCG as an order selector for almost six years, so if I was a bad employee and not meeting the work performance standards, WCG should have given me written warnings or reprimands. If WCG does not have this kind of written documentation, then WCG, or Ms. Martin, has no evidence to support their allegations. I then told the mediator about the bed race team that I put together with my white co-workers to show him that I did get along with my white co-workers. I said to myself, "I was smiling because like an athlete competing, WCG had just shown me that they could not stop me from winning this lawsuit."

The mediator said I met my prima facie burden and then told Ms. Martin, "WCG is taking a big risk if Judge Tanner hears this case based on what Mr. Stroman has just told me." Then McGavick called for a time out and took Mr. Lee and me to another room where McGavick wanted me to settle for $10,000.00. Mr. Lee started arguing with McGavick about the document that I had signed. This is when Mr. Lee got mad at McGavick, and told McGavick that he had sold me out. Mr. Lee then left the room and the building. As I got up to leave with Mr. Lee, McGavick tried again to convince me to accept $10,000. I just laughed at him and followed Mr. Lee out of the building and both of us went to Mr. Lee's house.

From the many nights I spent at Mr. Lee's house reading and interpreting the EEOC manual and the case law that was in the manual pertaining to complaints filed under Title VII, I felt confident that WCG could not produce a legitimate business reason why I should not have received the scheduling office training. From the case law that was in the manual, I read how some employers proved that an employee was not performing his or her job functions in a satisfactory matter, which led to the employee being terminated. In these cases, the employer was able to produce written warnings or reprimands showing that the employee was informed that he or she was not meeting performance standards. Additionally, the written warnings or reprimands stated specifically what the employee needed to do in order to correct the deficiencies; and if the deficiencies were not corrected the employee would receive further discipline, including termination. I knew WCG did not have this type of evidence to support their allegations that I had a poor job performance record. While WCG might have convinced the WSHRC investigators to believe that my complaints were not worthy of investigation, the 39.1 meeting federal mediator was not persuaded by WCG's position. He did not believe that I was a bad employee who could not get along with the white order selectors, and was not performing my job functions as an order selector in a satisfactory manner according to the collective bargaining agreement. Additionally, I felt confident in the knowledge I learned[16] that without any written warnings or reprimands WCG and its attorneys could not convince a federal judge that my work performance as an order selector was the reason they did not

---

[16] From the EEOC manual and the case law that was in the manual.

allow me the same opportunity for the on-the-job training in the scheduling office as the white employees.

On **July 2, 1987**, after reading the affidavits submitted by both sides, Federal District Judge Jack Tanner denied the WCG motion for summary judgment **(see exhibit 5)** without any written findings of fact on the WCG motion.[17] My case was scheduled to go to court four weeks later. Now I would have a chance to tell the federal court what I experienced while working at WCG.[18]

After the summary judgment ruling, Hugh McGavick really started to act funny (strange). At a meeting in his office, he started telling me that Judge Tanner did not know what he was doing, and he should have granted WCG's motion for summary judgment. McGavick then said that I only won the summary judgment motion because both Judge Tanner and I were black. It now seemed to me that McGavick did not care that I had a witness to establish that WCG's agent, Willie Mosley, and the WCG attorneys were not truthful about the *November 1, 1985 document.*

---

[17] According to Barron's Law Dictionary findings of fact are "factual determinations made by the trier of fact (court [judge] or jury) . . . based upon the evidence which has been presented to it."

[18] If WCG would have convinced Judge Tanner at the outset that I effectively waived my Title VII claims then WCG would have been confined to the terms of the November 1, 1985 document (i.e. information given out limited to date of hire, rate of pay, and journeyman status) then there would not have been a trial. Since this did not happen, WCG was not restricted to the terms of the November 1, 1985 document and could use any information they had related to my employment, to prove at trial, that the company did not discriminate against me. In addition, I would be able to show that WCG did not treat me equally to white employees when it came to having the same opportunity to receive training in the scheduling office.

At most of the meetings with McGavick, I had Mr. Lee with me. Mr. Lee and McGavick went back a long way since they both dealt with employment discrimination, Mr. Lee at the administration level and McGavick as a trial attorney. Mr. Lee's high respect for McGavick was the reason I asked McGavick if he would represent me. When McGavick said that Judge Tanner did not know what he was doing when he denied WCG's summary judgment motion, I asked, "Why are you saying this when you did a good job on your motion of opposition to the WCG motion for summary judgment that you filed in court?" To which McGavick responded,

> Yes, I did do a good job that got you over the summary judgment hurdle, but Judge Tanner should have granted summary judgment to WCG, and if I win at trial, the Ninth Circuit Court of Appeals is going to rule against me based on this *November 1, 1985 document.*

I then said, "Is that why you filed an unsigned affidavit from my friend Dave? Then I would have no witness to what I said to Mosley over the phone?" In addition, I stated to him, "What evidence did WCG produce to show that I knowingly, voluntarily, and intentionally waived my rights to sue WCG?" McGavick did not respond to my questions. He just said that I only won at the summary judgment because Judge Tanner and I were black.

When he started talking like this, Mr. Lee and I got upset and told McGavick to put in writing how legally, Judge Tanner did not know what he was doing with regards to WCG's summary judgment motion. McGavick did put his views on paper and mailed them to me. When I read McGavick's letter, the case law that he cited in the letter said, *"It is the defendant's burden to show the trial court Judge that the plaintiff voluntarily and knowingly intended to waive his or her federal rights.*" I knew WCG could not do this. McGavick also added that Judge Tanner and I being black was the reason Judge Tanner denied WCG's motion for summary judgment. After reading this, I became very upset and went to the federal courthouse with McGavick's letter, and said, "I want to see Judge Tanner."

Of course, I knew that no one was going to let an upset individual talk to a federal Judge, so I recited some of what McGavick said in this letter and left a copy of the letter for Judge Tanner. I then went home and called both Mr. Lee and McGavick telling them what I had just done. Mr. Lee was okay with it, but I could tell by McGavick's voice that he was concerned. After Judge Tanner denied WCG's motion for summary judgment on July 2, 1987, WCG filed a motion for reconsideration of their summary judgment. **On August 4, 1987**, Judge Tanner issued an order stating that he would hear oral arguments on WCG's reconsideration motion for summary judgment on **August 7, 1987 (see exhibit 6)**. A reconsideration motion is a request for the trial court judge to review the evidence submitted during the summary judgment motion, and hear legal arguments from the attorneys on the evidence submitted, as to why the summary judgment motion must be granted, or must be denied.

At this time, the only evidence on file with the court pertaining to the summary judgment motion was Willie Mosley's affidavit, my affidavit, and excerpts from my deposition. McGavick never did get an affidavit from my friend Dave Kehoi, even though McGavick referred to him in the conclusion part of his memorandum in opposition to WCG's summary judgment motion.

At the pre-trial hearing, which was a little over a week before the trial was to start and before the oral arguments on WCG's reconsideration motion, McGavick started trying to explain the letter that I left at the courthouse. Judge Tanner took his glasses off and looked McGavick right in his eyes and said to him that he did not read the letter, and that he had the office worker put the letter in a sealed envelope. Judge Tanner held up the sealed envelope so everybody at the pre-trial hearing could see it and said that it would be part of the court's record. (**) Judge Tanner then said to McGavick, "You should have known better, and you are still going to have to represent Mr. Stroman." He put his glasses back on and said to both attorneys, "Since there has not been any settlement between the parties I will see you at oral arguments on the defendant's motion for reconsideration." Judge Tanner then left the room. After the meeting, McGavick wanted to talk to me. Mr. Lee and I believed McGavick had been trying to sell me out, because he knew that I had evidence to prove my case of race discrimination against this big white corporation and witnesses to prove that WCG was not telling the truth pertaining to the *November 1, 1985 document.* I had nothing to say to him, so I left.

EXHIBIT #2

IN THE UNITED STATES DISTRICT COURT
FOR THE WESTERN DISTRICT OF WASHINGTON AT TACOMA

GRADY M. STROMAN,   )
)
                    Plaintiff,   )   C86-528T
)   NO.
          vs.   )
)
WEST COAST GROCERY COMPANY, a   )   COMPLAINT
Washington corporation,   )
)
                    Defendant.   )
_____)

COMES NOW, Plaintiff, and alleges and that:

I.

This Court has jurisdiction pursuant to 28 U.S.C. §§ 1331 and
1343, as well as pendant jurisdiction over State law claims.

II.

All acts complained of occurred in Pierce County, within the
Western District of Washington.

III.

Plaintiff, GRADY M. STROMAN, is a Black male.

IV.

Plaintiff has exhausted his administrative remedies.

V.

Defendant is a Washington corporation doing business in Pierce
County within the Western District of Washington.

COMPLAINT - 1

The Law Offices of

McGavick
& McGavick

250 Old City Hall
625 Commerce Street
P.O. Box 1877
Tacoma, Wa 98401

Tac. 206-572-6677
Sea. 206 838-2484

VI.

Plaintiff was an employee of Defendant from January 1980 through November 1985.

VII.

On or about April 11, 1984, Plaintiff applied for a supervisory position, which was given to a less qualified White individual, with less seniority.

VIII.

Plaintiff had previously frequently requested training in order to facilitate his advancement.

IX.

Plaintiff was told that he would not receive training until he demonstrated that he could get along with White employees.

X.

White employees received training without having to demonstrate that they can get along with Black employees.

XI.

Charles Young, a company official, told another Black employee, that Plaintiff would not be promoted because of his physical size, which would be intimidating to White employees he would have to supervise.

XII.

Defendant retaliated against Plaintiff after he filed the original charge of discrimination in July 1984.

XIII.

During December 1984, Plaintiff was denied sick leave in a

COMPLAINT - 2

The Law Offices of

McGavick
& McGavick

250 Old City Hall
625 Commerce Street
P.O. Box 1877
Tacoma, Wa 98401

Tac. 206-572-6677
Sea. 206 838-2484

discriminatory fashion.

XIV.

On or about March 31, 1985, Plaintiff was denied Union representation, after he had requested such representation, and was found to be insubordinate and was accordingly suspended.

XV.

Plaintiff grieved the preceding incident, and had it resolved in his favor at the National Labor Relations Board.

XVI.

In July 1985, Plaintiff was denied an opportunity to interview for a supervisory position for which he was qualified.

XVII.

The preceding incidents demonstrate Race discrimination and retaliation against Plaintiff for having opposed racial discrimination.

XVIII.

Plaintiff was on medical leave of absence from August 5, 1985 through November 1, 1985. This leave was as a result of distress and demands being placed on Plaintiff at the workplace, in large part due to discriminatory treatment.

XIX.

On or about October 3, 1985, Plaintiff followed the directions of his health care provider, and resigned from employment at West Coast Grocery, giving up only his seniority rights.

42 U.S.C. § 1981

XX.

Plaintiff realleges Paragraphs I through XIX as though fully

COMPLAINT - 3

The Law Offices of

McGavick
& McGavick

250 Old City Hall
625 Commerce Street
P.O. Box 1877
Tacoma, Wa 98401

Tac. 206-572-6677
Sea. 206 838-2484

set forth herein, and further alleges that he has been purposefully subjected to different punishments, pains, penalties, and other exactions than White employees were subjected to.

XXI.

Title VII

Plaintiff realleges Paragraphs I through XX as though fully set forth herein, and further alleges that Plaintiff has been the victim of intentional Race discrimination.

XXII.

Plaintiff has been the victim of intentional retaliation for having opposed Race discrimination.

XXIII.

Plaintiff has been subjected to different terms and conditions of employment than non-Black employees.

XXIV.

Plaintiff has been subjected to different terms and conditions of employment than employees who have not opposed racial discrimination.

XXV.

Plaintiff has been denied promotional opportunities in a racially discriminatory manner.

XXVI.

Plaintiff has been denied promotional opportunities because of his opposition to racial discrimination.

*****

*****

COMPLAINT - 4

The Law Offices of

McGavick
& McGavick

250 Old City Hall
625 Commerce Street
P.O. Box 1877
Tacoma, Wa 98401

Tac. 206-572-6677
Sea. 206 838-2484

XXVII.

RCW 49.60

Plaintiff realleges Paragraphs I through XXVI as though fully set forth herein, and further alleges that the preceding paragraphs establish Race discrimination and retaliation for having opposed Race discrimination.

XXVIII.

Constructive Discharge

Plaintiff realleges Paragraphs I through XXVII as though fully set forth herein.

XXIX.

The hostile work environment deteriorated to the point that Plaintiff was under so much stress and pressure that he was constructively discharged from his employment in November 1985.

XXX.

As a direct and proximate result of the discriminatory, retaliatory and constructive discharge of Defendant, Plaintiff has suffered, and will continue to suffer, ongoing damages and injury.

WHEREFORE, Plaintiff prays for judgment against Defendant, as follows:

1.   Declare that Defendant has violated 42 U.S.C. § 1981, Title VII, and RCW 49.60.

2.   Award Plaintiff actual and punitive damages for violations of 42 U.S.C. § 1981.

3.   Award Plaintiff actual damages and back pay for violations of Title VII and RCW 49.60.

COMPLAINT - 5

The Law Offices of

McGavick
& McGavick

250 Old City Hall
625 Commerce Street
P.O. Box 1877
Tacoma, Wa 98401

Tac. 206-572-6677
Sea. 206 838-2484

4. Award Plaintiff, in the alternative, reinstatement with retroactive seniority and benefits, or front pay in lieu of returning to a proven hostile environment.

5. Award Plaintiff actual and compensatory damages for violations of RCW 49.60.

6. Award Plaintiff actual and compensatory damages for constructive discharge.

7. Award Plaintiff attorney's fees and costs.

8. Award Plaintiff such other and further relief as the Court may deem just and appropriate.

DATED this ___30___ day of July, 1986.

_____
HUGH J. McGAVICK
Attorney for Plaintiff

COMPLAINT - 6/and last

The Law Offices of

McGavick
& McGavick

250 Old City Hall
625 Commerce Street
P.O. Box 1877
Tacoma, Wa 98401

Tac. 206-572-6677
Sea. 206 838-2484

EXHIBIT #3

THE HONORABLE JACK E. TANNER

FILED _____ LODGED
RECEIVED

JUN 15 1987

CLERK U.S. DISTRICT COURT
WESTERN DISTRICT OF WASHINGTON AT TACOMA
BY _____ DEPUTY

UNITED STATES DISTRICT COURT
WESTERN DISTRICT OF WASHINGTON
AT TACOMA

GRADY M. STROMAN,)
)
            Plaintiff,)   NO. C86-528T
)
      vs.)
)   PLAINTIFF'S MEMORANDUM IN
WEST COAST GROCERY COMPANY,)   OPPOSITION TO DEFENDANT'S
)   SUMMARY JUDGMENT MOTION
            Defendant.)
)
_____)

COMES NOW the Plaintiff, by and through his Attorney of
Record, and submits this Memorandum in Opposition to the
Defendant's Summary Judgment Motion.

FACTUAL BACKGROUND

I

Defendant herein moves for Summary Judgement based on the
preclusive effect of the sixth provision of an Agreement, dated
November 1, 1985. That contractual provision reads as follows:

"These terms represent a full and final settlement of
any and all claims arising out of Mike's employment
with West Coast Grocery."

However, it is Plaintiff's contention that the sixth

MEMORANDUM IN OPPOSITION TO SUMMARY JUDGMENT - 1

The Law Offices of   250 Old City Hall
                      625 Commerce Street,
                      P.O. Box 1877
McGavick   Tacoma, Wa 98401
& McGavick   Tel 206-572-6677

provision of the Agreement is not preclusive based upon the totality of the circumstances, as demonstrated in the arguments below. It is also Plaintiff's contention that the Agreement is not a "Settlement Agreement," as averred by Defendant.

Plaintiff further takes exception to several statements averred in the "Factual Background" section of Defendant's Memorandum in Support of Motion for Summary Judgment. Those exceptions are addressed in the following Arguments, and in the Affidavit of Plaintiff, appended hereto.

ISSUE

II

Whether, under Washington State contract law and Federal statutory law, Plaintiff's lawsuit is barred, and Summary Judgment is appropriate, based on the Agreement, dated November 1, 1985. .

LEGAL ARGUMENTS

III

THE STANDARD FOR GRANTING DEFENDANT'S SUMMARY JUDGMENT MOTION DOES NOT EXIST IN THE CASE AT BAR.

The grant of Summary Judgment is appropriate if it appears, after reviewing the evidence in a light most favorable to the opposing party, that there is no genuine issue of material fact, and that the moving party is entitled to judgment as a matter of law. Lew v. Kona Hospital, 765 F.2d 1420, 1423 (9th Cir. 1985); and Celotex Corp. v. Catrett, --- U.S. ---, 106 S.Ct. 2548 (1986).

MEMORANDUM IN OPPOSITION TO SUMMARY JUDGMENT - 2

The Law Offices of

McGavick

250 Old City Hall
625 Commerce Street
P.O. Box 1677
Tacoma, Wa 98401

Here, in its Summary Judgment Motion, Defendant contends (1) that Plaintiff initiated the concept and discussion of the Agreement, (2) that Plaintiff and Defendant's agent, Mr. Willie Mosely, thoroughly discussed each of the six provisions contained in the Agreement, and (3) that Plaintiff voluntarily and knowingly entered into the Agreement.

Conversely, Plaintiff contends (1) that Defendant formulated and extended the basic provisions of the Agreement to all of its employees at a time it was experiencing the loss of a contract; (2) that Defendant's agent represented to Plaintiff that the Agreement at issue here was basically the same as that proffered by Defendant to all of its employees; and (3) that Defendant fraudently, purposefully, willfully, and knowingly mislead and induced Plaintiff into signing the Agreement by Defendant's agent gaining Plaintiff's trust.

In Meissner v. Simpson Timber Co., 69 Wn.2d 949, 421 P.2d 674 (1966), the Court stated that:

> It is the duty of the trial court to consider all evidence and all reasonable inferences therefrom most favorable to the nonmoving party. Id., at 951.

In Washington State, it has also been held that:

> A summary judgment cannot be entered if there be a genuine issue as to any material fact. Fraud will vitiate the contract.

Coson v. Roehl, 63 Wn.2d 834, 387 P.2d 541 (1963).

Since this is a Summary Judgment Motion, all facts and inferences must be drawn in favor of the non-movant, and the Court is not permitted to weigh the evidence, pass upon the credibility or speculate as to the ultimate findings of fact.

MEMORANDUM IN OPPOSITION TO SUMMARY JUDGMENT - 3

The Law Offices of

McGovick
& McGovick

250 Old City Hall
625 Commerce Street
P.O. Box 1877
Tacoma, Wa 98401

Tac. 206-572-6677
Con 206-838-2484

See, Pepper and Tanner, Inc. v. Shamrock Broadcasting, Inc., 563 F.2d 391, 393, (9th Cir. 1977).

The above-delineated positions and postulations of Plaintiff and Defendant make clear that the Parties differ substantially on the material matter of how the Agreement came about, and what its originally-agreed upon purpose was to be. Those differences constitute the existence of a genuine issue of material fact. Plaintiff further avers fraud and misrepresentation were employed by Defendant to induce him into signing the Agreement.

Therefore, the diametrically-opposing statements of the Parties, and the alleged fraudulent conduct by Defendant, unequivocally bar the granting of a Summary Judgment.

IV

THE SIXTH PROVISION OF THE AGREEMENT IS VOIDABLE BY PLAINTIFF ON CONTRACT PRINCIPLES.

Reiterating, the sixth provision of the Agreement, which Defendant relies upon to support its Summary Judgment Motion, reads as follows:

> "These terms represent a full and final settlement of
> any and all claims arising out of Mike's employment
> with West Coast Grocery."

MISREPRESENTATION AND FRAUD

In Washington State, it is clear that a contract may be either reformed or rescinded when the contract is based upon a material misrepresentation. In such instances, proof of fraud is not necessary to show the misrepresentation. Kruger v. Redi-Brew Corp., 9 Wn. App. 322, 511 P.2d 1405 (1973); and Alexander

MEMORANDUM IN OPPOSITION TO SUMMARY JUDGMENT - 4

The Law Offices of

McGavick
& McGavick

250 Old City Hall
625 Commerce Street
P.O. Box 1877
Tacoma, Wa 98401

Tac. 206-572-6677
Sea. 206 838-2484

Myers & Co. v. Hopke, 88 Wn.2d 449, 565 P.2d 80 (1977).
Accordingly, whether Defendant's agent, Mr. Willie Mosley, acted
intentionally or unintentionally in representing the effect and
meaning of the sixth provision to Plaintiff, the outcome
constitutes "fraud in the inducement." Maki v. Aluminum Building
Products, 73 Wn.2d 23 (1968). This is evidenced by the fact that
Mr. Mosley's employer, the Defendant herein, now seeks to deny
Plaintiff his Title VII statutory rights based on the combined
facts that first, Mr. Mosley's statements induced Plaintiff to
sign the Agreement, and second, Plaintiff never would have
knowingly entered into a contract that would summarily terminate
his long-standing racial employment discrimination claims against
Defendant.

Thus, Plaintiff contends that Defendant, through its agent,
Mr. Mosley, misrepresented to him the effect of the
aforementioned provision in the Agreement, although Mr. Mosely
now contends otherwise. These opposing statements of fact
amounts to a genuine issue of material facts, which cannot be
resolved by a Summary Judgment Motion, as Defendant seeks to do
here.

REFORMATION AND RESCISSION

Even if the Court were so inclined to grant the Summary
Judgment Motion sought by Defendant, it must first consider
Plaintiff's contention that reformation or rescission of the
contract's sixth provision is the only appropriate action this
Court should take on that matter, since:

MEMORANDUM IN OPPOSITION TO SUMMARY JUDGMENT - 5

The Law Offices of

McGavick
& McGavick

250 Old City Hall
625 Commerce Street
P.O. Box 1877
Tacoma, Wa 98401

Tac. 206-572-6677
Sea. 206 838-2484

Reformation will be granted when there is a mistake on the part of one of the parties as to the content of a document and there is fraud or inequitable conduct on the part of the other party. It is not determinative that the mistaken party could have noticed the discrepancy between his understanding and the written agreement by reading the document. Mitchell International Enterprises, Inc. v. Daley, 33 Wn.App 562, 656 P.2d 1113 (1983). See also, Gammel v. Diethelm, 59 Wn.2d 504, 368 P.2d 718 (1962); and Cavanaugh v. Brewington, 3 Wn. App. 757, 477 P.2d 644 (1970).

Finally, reformation or rescission of a contract also is appropriate when one party to a contract is cognizant that the other party knows that the other has entered into the agreement on a mistaken belief. In re: Estate of Greer, 29 Wn. App. 822,

Here, Plaintiff clearly relied upon the interpretation of the sixth provision provided by Defendant's agent, Mr. Mosley; and it is equally clear that Plaintiff would not have entered into the contract, as written, but for Mr. Mosley's fraudulent misrepresentations as to the effect of the contract. Thus, Plaintiff's mistaken belief of, and consent to the effect of the sixth provision was fraudulently induced by Defendant's agent's influence over Plaintiff, and Defendant knew of Plaintiff's mistaken belief, since it purposefully caused that belief to come about.

Therefore, under Greer, supra., Defendant is prohibited from inducing a mistaken belief, and then taking advantage of that mistaken belief.

UNCONSCIONABILITY AND UNDUE INFLUENCE

The doctrine of unconscionability requires scrutiny of the totality of the circumstances that surrounded the transaction in

MEMORANDUM IN OPPOSITION TO SUMMARY JUDGMENT - 6

The Law Offices of

McGavick
& McGavick

250 Old City Hall
625 Commerce Street
P.O. Box 1877
Tacoma, Wa 98401

Tac. 206-572-6677
Sea. 206 838-2484

question at the time the contract is made. Christiansen

Brothers, v. State, 90 Wn.2d 872, 877, 586 P.2d 840, 845 (1978);

and Jeffrey v. Weintraub, 32 Wn.App. 536, 649 P.2d 914 (1982).

See also Restatement (Second) of Contracts, Section 208 (1981).

Significantly, in Schroeder v. Fageol Motors, Inc., 86

Wn.2d 256, 544 P.2d 20 (1975), the Court discerned two distinct

forms of unconscionability. There, it said that:

> Substantive unconscionability involves those cases where
> a clause or term in the contract is alleged to be one-
> sided or overly harsh, while procedural unconscionability
> relates to impropriety during the process of forming a
> contract. (Emphases added.)

Further, in dicta, the Schroeder Court stated that "a court

is not authorized to dispose of [the issue of unconscionability]

under the rules governing summary judgment." Id., at 262.

In this case, Plaintiff, a Black man, alleges in his

Affidavit that he was tricked and mislead into signing the

Agreement based on assurances given to him by someone he trusted

(Mr. Mosley), who also is a Black man, and whom lead Plaintiff to

reasonably believe that he (Mr. Mosley) was looking out for and

acting in the best interest of Plaintiff. This misleading action

by Mr. Mosley constitutes undue influence. Accordingly, when a

contract is made when one of the parties lacked free consent, or

signs as a result of the other party's undue influence the

contract is vitiated. Maki, supra, and Ferguson v. Jeans, 27

Wn.App. 562, 619 P.2d 369 (1980). Thus, under Schroeder, the bad

acts and unclean hands of Defendant and its agent prohibit

Defendant from now coming into Court to seek relief without a

MEMORANDUM IN OPPOSITION TO SUMMARY JUDGMENT -- 7

The Law Offices of

McGavick
& McGavick

250 Old City Hall
625 Commerce Street
P.O. Box 1877
Tacoma, Wa 98401

Tac. 206-572-6677
Sea. 206 838-2484

full adjudication on the merits and a finding of facts by the factfinders.

UNILATERAL MISTAKE

A unilateral mistake is grounds for either reformation or rescission of a contract. Thus, the sixth provision of the Agreement is not enforceable against Plaintiff.

In Seafirst National Bank v. Earl, 17 Wn.App. 830, 565 P.2d 1215 (1977), Petition for Review Denied 89 Wn.2d 1017, the Court reviewed a lease agreemenrt where one party had knowledge of a material portion of the Agreement, and the other party did not. The Court held that "if one party has no independent knowledge and accepted another's analysis and opinion [of the effect of the Agreement], the mistake is unilateral." (Citations omitted.) The Court considered several factors, including that the document was prepared by the party seeking its enforcement (as with the case at bar). Since the party seeking to enforce the contract sought equitable relief, the Court stated that when those powers were invoked, the Court would give close scrutiny to the result to be obtained through the invocation of those powers. United States v. Systrom-Donner Corp., 486 F.2d 249 (9th Cir. 1973); and Seafirst National Bank, supra., at 837.

In Loeb Rhoades, Horn Blower Co. v. Keen, 28 Wn.App. 499 (1981), the Court stated that:

> Where there is a unilateral mistake, Courts will not in-
> voke their equitable powers to aid the party who was the
> sole cause of his misfortune. (Citations, including the
> Seafirst National Bank v. Earl case, supra., omitted).
> The rule is contra if the other party knows of the mis-
> take or is charged with knowledge of it.

MEMORANDUM IN OPPOSITION TO SUMMARY JUDGMENT - 8

The Law Offices of

McGovick
& McGovick

250 Old City Hall
625 Commerce Street
P.O. Box 1877
Tacoma, Wa 98401

Toc. 206-572-6677
Sea. 206 838-2484

In the case at hand, Plaintiff reasonbly relied upon the intrepretation of the effect of the Agreement's sixth provision that was given to him by Defendant's agent, Mr. Mosley. Consequently, the unilateral mistake made by Plaintiff is not chargeable against him, since the mistake was caused by Defendant.

V

Public Policy Principles makes the Sixth Provision of the Agreement Void as Against Public Policy.

VOLUNTARILY AND KNOWINGLY

The inclusion of the sixth provision into the Agreement is not enforceable because it is contrary to public policy. In order to be valid and enforceable, the Agreement must be voluntary and knowing. The United States Supreme Court has previously held that "a statutory right conferred on a private party, but affecting the public interest, may not be waived or released if such waiver or release contravenes the statutory policy." Brooklyn Savings v. O'Neil, 65 S.Ct. 895, 900-01 (19—).

In this case, the relevant public policy is embodied in a statutory scheme, Title VII. Also in this case, Defendant alleges that Plaintiff has waived his rights to Title VII remedies for alleged violations of that statutory scheme by Defendant.

In Alexander v. Gardner-Denver Co., 415 U.S. 36, 94 S.Ct. 1011, 39 L.Ed.2d 147 (1974), as in Brooklyn Savings, supra., the

MEMORANDUM IN OPPOSITION TO SUMMARY JUDGMENT - 9

The Law Offices of
McGovick
& McGovick

250 Old City Hall
625 Commerce Street
P.O. Box 1877
Tacoma, Wa 98401

Toc. 206-572-6677
Sea 206 838-2484

Supreme Court stated that an employee may waive his cause of action under Title VII as part of a voluntary settlement. But at footnote 15, the Court noted that:

> [The parties] did not enter into a voluntary settlement expressly conditioned on a waiver of [the employee's] cause of action under Title VII. In determining the effectiveness of any such waiver, a Court would have to determine at the outset that the employee's consent to the suit was voluntary and knowing. (Emphasis added.) Id., 415 U.S. at 51-52, 39 L.Ed.2d at 160.

Thus, Alexander makes "...clear that there can be no...waiver of an employee's rights under Title VII." Alexander, supra., 415 U.S. at 51-52, 39 L.Ed.2d 147, 160. Alexander has been cited approvingly by the Washington State Supreme Court in Reese v. Sears, Roebuck & Co., 107 Wn.2d 563, 573 (1987).

Further, in Hederman v. George, 35 Wn.2d 357 (1949), the Court stated that a "...contract, which is contrary to the terms and policy of an express legislative enactment is illegal and unenforceable." Id. at 362. Thus, since it is clear that the sixth provision of the Agreement, in effect, attempts to negate Plaintiff's Federal statutory rights under Title VII, Defendant is equitably estopped from enforcing that unconscionable provision. Otherwise, a Summary Judgment would have the effect of circumventing a national policy of prohibiting racial discrimination in the workplace.

In a case not unlike the present one, a Federal District Court was presented with a factual issue on whether a purported "release" had been given knowingly. The Court stated that:

MEMORANDUM IN OPPOSITION TO SUMMARY JUDGMENT - 10

The Law Offices of

McGavick
& McGavick

250 Old City Hall
625 Commerce Street
P.O. Box 1877
Tacoma, Wa 98401

Toc. 206-572-6677

Plaintiffs assert that the terms of the agreement negotiated with them were not binding because the company was in full possession of the facts, and the individuals were and still are not. On the record we hold that there exists a factual dispute as to the validity and effect of the release. Therefore, the motion by [defendant] for summary judgment against the individual Plaintiffs is denied. Johnson v. Vancouver Plywood Co., 16 FEP Cases 1537, 1539 (W.D. La. 1976).

Thus, as in Johnson, Summary Judgment is inappropriate here on the waiver of a statutory right.

In Runyan v. National Cash Register Corp., 787 F2d 1039, the Court stated that a "...Court should not allow employers to compromise underlying policies of [discrinmination lasws] by taking advantage of a superior bargaining position or by overreaching." Id., at 1044-45. And in Felty v. Graves-Humphreys Co., 785 F.2d 516, 520 (4th Cir. 1986), the Court stated that "[t]he remedial goals of [discrimination laws] cannot be circumvented by an employer's coercive pratices, no matter how stuble the form."

Applying the Runyan and Felty cases to the case at bar, is is clear that Defendant cannot rely upon the November 1, 1985 Agreement to secure the Summary Judgment, as it would contravene public policy, and compromise the equity powers of this Court. Therefore, the Motion must be denied.

CONCLUSION

In order to be valid and enforceable, the Agreement relied upon by Defendant to support its Summary Judgment Motion must have been entered into knowingly and voluntarily. As the Affidavits of Plaintiff and David Kehoi make clear, Plaintiff

MEMORANDUM IN OPPOSITION TO SUMMARY JUDGMENT - 11

The Law Offices of

McGavick
& McGavick

250 Old City Hall
625 Commerce Street
P.O. Box 1877
Tacoma, Wa 98401

Tac. 206-572-6677
Sea. 206-838-2484

never considered giving-up his Title VII statutory right to seek equitable and other relief for the racially-discriminatory injuries inflicted upon him by Defendant. Therefore, it can be objectively concluded that Plaintiff did not knowingly and voluntarily enter into the sixth provision of the Agreement, and that the procuring of his agreement thereto could only have been accomplished by fraud, deceit, misrepresentation, or some other unconscionable action on the part of Defendant and/or Defendant's agent. Further, the postulations of Defendant's agent, Mr. Mosley, is suspect since Mr. Mosley remains in the employ of Defendant and has reason to make other than truthful statements to protect his job.

For the foregoing reasons, Defendant's Motion for Summary Judgment should be denied.

DATED this __15th__ day of June, 1987.

                                    MCGAVICK & MCGAVICK

                                    HUGH J. MCGAVICK
                                    Attorney for Plaintiff

MEMORANDUM IN OPPOSITION TO SUMMARY JUDGMENT - 12

The Law Offices of   250 Old City Hall
                          625 Commerce Street
McGavick   P.O. Box 1877
& McGavick   Tacoma, Wa 98401

                          Tac. 206-572-6677

EXHIBIT #4

HONORABLE JACK E. TANNER

IN THE UNITED STATES DISTRICT COURT
FOR THE WESTERN DISTRICT OF WASHINGTON AT TACOMA

GRADY M. STROMAN,   )
)
                    Plaintiff,   )   NO. C86-528T
)
          vs.   )   AFFIDAVIT OF PLAINTIFF
)   IN OPPOSITION TO DEFENDANT'S
WEST COAST GROCERY COMPANY,   )   MOTION FOR SUMMARY JUDGMENT
)
                    Defendant.   )
_____)

STATE OF WASHINGTON   )
) ss.
County of Pierce   )

          COMES NOW GRADY M. STROMAN and deposes and says that:

          I am the Plaintiff herein and competent to testify to the

matters set forth below.

          I make this Affidavit substantially in opposition to the

Affidavit submitted by Willie Mosley in support of Defendant's Motion

for Summary Judgment.

          When I first contacted Willie Mosley about the layoff

possibility, he told me I would have to sign papers which set forth

the terms and conditions of the layoff. I had no problem with that.

          Mosley says he read the conditions over the phone to me. I

deny that. The only things he advised me of were that I would be

giving up my rights for recall and seniority, and in return I would

The Law Offices of
McGavick
& McGavick

250 Old City Hall
625 Commerce Street
P.O. Box 1877
Tacoma, Wa 98401
Tac. 206-572-6677

receive uncontested Employment Security Department unemployment
benefits. He never told me I would have to give up my Washington
State Human Rights charges because he knew I would not have signed if
those strings had been attached.

   I had a job opportunity lined up in California at the time
these negotiations were going on with West Coast Grocery. During my
medical leave of absence from August 1985 through November 1, 1985, I
had gone to California, my original home, and performed a job search.
I thought I had successfully found a job, and had already decided and
was desirous of leaving West Coast Grocery. Therefore, the layoff
allowed me unemployment benefits to help during the transition.

   I originally called Willie Mosley on or about October 31, 1985.
A friend of mine, Dave Quoxite was present and overheard my part of
that phone conversation. He has made an Affidavit in opposition to
Defendant's Motion as well.

   I was released to return to work on November 1, 1985.
Scheduled days off were November 1 and November 2, 1985. On Sunday,
November 3, 1985, I reported to work, as that was my first assigned
work day after my medical leave of absence. I spoke with my
supervisor, Mr. John Lee, to get a time card. This occurred in the
scheduling office of West Coast Grocery. He advised me that he could
not let me work. I told Lee to get Willie Mosley on the phone, which
Lee did. Lee then walked out of the office. I could not see anyone
else in the room, although it is possible someone else was also
present.

   On the preceding Thursday and Friday, I checked with the

The Law Offices of   250 Old City Hall
                        625 Commerce Street
                        P.O. Box 1877
McGavick   Tacoma, Wa 98401
& McGavick

Employment Security Department to find out if I would be eligible
under these terms. That was in the Lakewood Office. I was not
certain after speaking with the Employment Security Department if I
would be eligible. During my phone conversation from West Coast
Grocery to Willie Mosley on November 3, 1985, I advised Mr. Mosley of
what I had learned at the Employment Security Department. He
reassured me that I was qualified and eligible. This took up the bulk
of our 5-8 minute conversation. He told me all I would have to do is
give up my seniority rights and right of recall. I told him that that
was all I was giving up, and he agreed. He told me to come in the
next day to sign. Mosley never said anything to me about giving up
any other rights.

On November 4, 1985, I went into the Operations Office at about
10:00 a.m. Mr. Mosley concluded a meeting he was having with another
employee, and said "Come on in, Michael." No other words were spoken
as the document was handed to me. Dave Hamlin's signature was already
on the document. I took the document, read it, and no other words
were spoken. I read the complete frame, and stated, "I'm not sure
about this last one, Willie." Mosley did not say "That I did not see
anything that bothered (me)." Affidavit of Mosley at Page 4,
Paragraph 13. Mosley did not respond. He did not say "You are giving
up all claims against West Coast Grocery." Mosley Affidavit at Page
4, Paragraph 13. He did not say that signing meant "No more suits."
Mosley Affidavit at Page 4, Paragraph 15. I said, "Well, I guess
trust has got to start somewhere." Mosely responded, "Well, you can
trust us, Michael, because all we're asking is for full-time employees

The Law Offices of   250 Old City Hall
                          625 Commerce Street
                          P.O. Box 1877
McGovick   Tacoma, Wa 98401
& McGovick
                          Tac. 206-572-6677

to give up seniority rights so they can collect unemployment." In direct contradiction of his statement at Page 3, Paragraph 11, that he advised me that I could take it to an attorney, Mosely mentioned nothing about an attorney. He did not emphasize that no one was trying to force me to sign this document. Affidavit of Mosely at Page 4, Paragraph 12.

I signed the document, handed it to Mosely, who went out to make a copy, returned, and wished me good luck. This meeting lasted five (5) minutes maximum. I went immediately to the Employment Security Department to do the paperwork.

Had Hamlin been there, I would have had a witness present, because of my prior experience with the company and my strong desire to always have equality in numbers in meetings. In fact, I was suspended because I refused to attend a meeting without a Union representative which led to a NLRB charge and a Washington State Human Rights charge.

With regard to that NLRB charge which was settled between the parties, on June 7, 1985 I was originally proffered a settlement agreement. The fourth paragraph of that document originally said "This constitutes full and final settlement of this charge and the subject of this charge will not be used by either party in any other action or proceeding." I revised that agreement when it was proffered to me to read as follows, "This constitutes full and final settlement of this charge involving the National Labor Relations Board." That is the language which was incorporated in the final document which I signed. Copies of those documents are attached as Exhibit A and B to

The Law Offices of

McGavick
& McGavick

250 Old City Hall
625 Commerce Street
P.O. Box 1877
Tacoma, Wa 98401
Inc. 206-572-6677

my Affidavit.

If I had thought that Paragraph 6 of the Settlement Agreement offered by West Coast Grocery which is the basis for this Motion would have precluded my Washington State Human Rights charges and subsequent lawsuit, I would have never signed them. I would not have signed them if he had told me I was waiving Washington State Human Rights, Title VII or RCW rights and remedies. The award of unemployment is totally disproportionate to the amount of injury, frustration, and damage I have suffered in this action.

Attached to the Affidavit of Elizabeth Pike Martin are two pages of excerpts from my deposition. Those do not give the Court the full flavor of what I was deposed about. For the Court's consideration are pages 130-39 are attached to show my consistent recitation of the events surrounding my signing the November 1, 1985 Settlement Agreement waiving my seniority and recall rights.

FURTHER AFFIANT SAYETH NAUGHT.

GRADY M. STROMAN

SUBSCRIBED AND SWORN to before me this 16th day of June, 1987.

NOTARY PUBLIC in and for the State of Washington, residing at Tacoma.

The Law Offices of

McGavick
& McGavick

250 Old City Hall
625 Commerce Street
P.O. Box 1877
Tacoma, WA 98401

EXHIBIT #5

IN THE UNITED STATES DISTRICT COURT
FOR THE WESTERN DISTRICT OF WASHINGTON
AT TACOMA

GRADY M. STROMAN,   )

               Plaintiff,   )   NO. C86-528T

    -vs-   )

WEST COAST GROCERY COMPANY,   )   ORDER

              Defendant.   )

THIS MATTER comes on before the above-entitled Court upon Defendant's
Motion for Summary Judgment.

Having considered the entirety of the records and file herein, it is now

ORDERED that Defendant's Motion for Summary Judgment is DENIED.

The clerk of the court is instructed to send uncertified copies of this Order
to all counsel of record.

DATED this _____2nd_____ day of JULY, 1987.

UNITED STATES DISTRICT JUDGE

EXHIBIT #6

ENTERED ON
AUG 5 1987
By Deputy

IN THE UNITED STATES DISTRICT COURT
FOR THE WESTERN DISTRICT OF WASHINGTON
AT TACOMA

GRADY M. STROMAN,   )
)
                Plaintiff,   )   NO. C86-528T
)
        -vs-   )
)
WEST COAST GROCERY,   )   ORDER
)
                Defendant.   )
_____

        THIS MATTER comes on before the above-entitled Court upon Defendant's

Motion to Shorten Time to Consider its Motion for Reconsideration of Defendant's

Motion for Summary Judgment.

        Having considered the entirety of the records and file herein, it is now

        ORDERED that Defendant's Motion to Shorten Time is GRANTED; and it is

further

        ORDERED that this Court shall hear oral argument on Defendant's Motion

for Reconsideration of its Motion for Summary Judgment, on Friday, the 7th day of

August, 1987 at 2:30 p.m., in Room 351.

        The clerk of the court is instructed to send uncertified copies of this Order

to all counsel of record.

        DATED this _____ day of August, 1987.

                        _____
                        UNITED STATES DISTRICT JUDGE

Chapter Twelve

Judge Tanner's Ruling

During the time when McGavick was acting as if he was selling me out, I had been talking to an individual about my case, someone who used to work for the EEOC in Seattle. He told me that he could not believe that neither the EEOC, nor the WSHRC had investigated my complaints, but he believed me that nothing had been done with my case by these two agencies. He then said that if I did have the evidence that I told him about, he knew of an attorney named Mike Gallagher in the Seattle area who would take my case. Therefore, I called McGavick and told him, "If you want to withdraw from my case, go ahead and file your motion, and I will be down to pick up all of my documents that I have given you." On **August 14, 1987**, the court granted McGavick's motion to withdraw as my attorney after Mike Gallagher filed his motion to become my new attorney. The oral argument date for WCG's reconsideration of their summary judgment was changed to **January 29, 1988**, and the trial date was re-scheduled for **March 21, 1988** (Again all three of the above can be found at the Federal Archive Building under Stroman v. West Coast Grocery). This meant I had to wait some time before I would go to trial.

As my new attorney, Gallagher wanted everything in McGavick's file pertaining to my case. So I went to McGavick's office to pick up my documents. He told me that I would have to go to a particular copying place and "pay to pick up my documents." I said, "You are refusing to give me the documents that I gave you pertaining to my allegations against WCG?" He said, "No, but if you want the documents, you will have to pay for them." I left his office and I then told my new attorney about this situation. Gallagher stated that he needs the documents that I gave to McGavick. So I paid to get the documents back from the copying place. Now I was convinced that McGavick was trying to stop me from suing WCG.

I later filed a complaint with the Washington State Bar Association against McGavick on this issue and regarding his statement that 'Judge Tanner did not know what he was doing' (surrounding WCG's summary judgment) and that 'I only won at the summary judgment motion because Judge Tanner and I were black.' The Washington State Bar Association ruled that McGavick did no wrong by making his remarks to me about Judge Tanner and myself, but did order that McGavick had to reimburse me for what I paid the copying company for my documents. McGavick was not punished for not returning my documents that I had given him pertaining to my case.

During the time period while I was waiting to go to court, my new attorney became familiar with my case and talked to my friends about the lay-off offer by Willie Mosley to the order selectors—something McGavick never did. For the reconsideration hearing, WCG did not produce any new evidence, they only resubmitted Willie Mosley's affidavit. However, my new attorney filed a memorandum in opposition to WCG's motion for reconsideration of their summary motion dated **January 25, 1988**, stating again that the WCG's agent "'Willie Mosley's version of events' lacks veracity and the defendant is precluded by contract from entering into an agreement with the plaintiff regarding his employment" (**see exhibit 7**). To show that Mosley 'lacked veracity' he filed affidavits, dated October 30, 1987, and January 14, 1988, from my two friends (Dan and Rich) who told me about the offer Willie Mosley made to the order selectors, which was new evidence for Judge Tanner to consider (**see exhibit 8**). These affidavits show that Mosley made a lay-off offer to the order selectors at WCG, and that none of the other order selectors had to waive their union recall rights, while I had to waive my union recall rights, which meant the document was discriminatory. In addition, my new attorney argued in his memorandum that this *November 1, 1985 document* violated the collective bargaining agreement. Under the collective bargaining agreement between WCG and the Union,

> The Employer agrees not to enter into any agreement or contract with his employees individually or collectively, which in any way conflicts with the terms and provisions of this agreement. Any such agreement shall be 'null and void.'

This means WCG's agents knew that they could not enter into an agreement or contract with me that required that I waive my union recall rights. WCG's agents had to know, based on contract law under the collective bargaining agreement, that such an agreement or contract would be "null and void." The collective bargaining agreement was also new evidence for Judge Tanner to consider.

There was no oral argument, and on **February 9, 1988**, Judge Tanner denied WCG's motion for reconsideration of their summary judgment without written findings (**see exhibit 9**). The evidence that I produced at the summary judgment level clearly showed that Mosley lacked credibility. Since there were no findings of fact, I believe Judge Tanner's decision to deny WCG's summary judgment was based on the lack of credibility of WCG and its agents. Additionally, he apparently believed it was a waste of valuable court time to make written findings on this fraudulent attempt by WCG and its agents to deceive him. Also, though I had already shown Judge Tanner that WCG's agents lacked credibility on the issue of the *November 1, 1985 document*, at trial both WCG and I would have the opportunity to convince him which one of us was more credible on the allegations of racial employment discrimination (violations of Title VII). If he believed WCG was more credible then he would make findings in favor of WCG on the allegations of violations of Title VII. Then no one would be able to ask about any findings concerning WCG's summary judgment motions. On the other hand, if he believed I was more credible then he would make findings in my favor on the allegations of violations of Title VII. Then there would be no need for findings on WCG's summary judgment motions unless WCG appealed to the Ninth Circuit and the Ninth Circuit remanded the case back to Judge Tanner to make findings on why he denied WCG's summary judgment motions.

On **March 21, 1988**, I finally went to trial to describe what I believe was racial discrimination treatment towards me while I was employed at WCG. When the trial first started, Judge Tanner said on the record that the trial would only cover the period while I worked at WCG, and that he did not want to hear anything that he had already denied at the summary judgment level "as a matter of law."

Finally, the trial began. I testified to what I believe was discrimination pertaining to the selection of individuals who were given the chance to be trained in the scheduling office and were later promoted to supervisory positions, and also about what I believe was retaliation against me by WCG because I filed a complaint of employment discrimination with the EEOC/WSHRC. All three of my WSHRC complaints were entered as exhibits during the trial (all three complaints are part of my record at the Federal Archive Building in Seattle, Washington).

My testimony about the retaliation mainly centered around WCG suspending me for insubordination when the Teamster Union filed a complaint with the National Labor Relations Board on my behalf against WCG, and because I was not interviewed for the last supervisory position for which I applied before going on my unpaid medical leave of absence. In addition, I had to read the *"Up from Slavery"* book when no other order selector had to read a book to receive the training in the schedule office and I had to come in on my off time to observe the operations of the schedule office without pay.

After I testified, Don Glaude testified that a group of black order selectors had a meeting with management to complain about the racial slurs on the bathroom walls. Additionally, Don testified that Charles Young treated them (the black order selectors who complained) more harshly than he treated the white warehouse workers. Don also testified that Charles told him that he had to work harder than the whites did because he was black and that was just the way it was. He also said certain people were 'hand-picked' by supervision to be trained in the scheduling office and that during his time of employment (while I was there) no black had ever received this training. He also testified that when he asked for the training in the scheduling office Charles told him that he was not ready.

After Don testified, James Caputo testified. He was the business representative and executive officer of Teamster Local 599. He testified about the labor agreement between WCG and the Union pertaining to written warnings, suspensions, and discharges that were not in accordance with the provisions of the agreement between WCG and the Union, and stated that any discipline that was not in accordance with the agreement rendered it invalid.

Lastly, my attorney called Dave Hamlin, who was the operation manager at WCG to testify. I believe Dave did not like me because I told him that I thought the selection of who was to be trained and given promotion opportunities was discriminatory. Dave admitted that he had discussions with me pertaining to training in the scheduling office and subsequent to one of those discussions, he prepared a letter to me containing hints or suggestions of things that I could do to qualify myself for the training in the scheduling office. Dave admitted he recommended that I should read a book by Booker T. Washington, called *"Up from Slavery."* He told me that he had not read the book before recommending it to me, but during the trial, he stated that he had read it prior to recommending it to me. My attorney pointed out that in the book on page 46 it states, "With few exceptions, the Negro youth must work harder, must perform his task even better than a white youth in order to secure recognition."

In addition, on page 63 it states:

I sometimes feel that almost the most valuable lesson I got from the Hampton Institute was in the use and value of the bath. I learned there for the first time some of its value, not only in keeping the body healthy, but also in inspiring self-respect and promoting virtue.

Lastly, on page 102 it states:

But no white American ever thinks that any other race is wholly civilized until he wears the white man's clothes, eats the white man's food, speaks the white man's language and professes the white man's religion.[19]

---

[19]   My attorney was reading from the book that was given to me by Dave, the page numbers are different from the book I referred to in my bibliography, but the quotes are the same in both books.

Dave admitted that even though he knew that I filed a complaint of racial employment discrimination against WCG he still recommended this book for me to read as good advice for working hard and getting ahead.

All during the two days of the trial, WCG's lead attorney, Mr. Whitters kept trying to argue that I waived my right to sue them. Each time Mr. Whitters tried to bring this issue up my attorney said, "Mr. Stroman disputes what WCG is arguing and has witnesses here to testify *that Mosley offered the lay off to full time employees.*" Furthermore, my attorney stated that the *November 1, 1985 document* violates the collective bargaining agreement that WCG has with the Union.[20]

Each time Mr. Whitters brought up the issue of the *November 1, 1985 document*, Judge Tanner responded that he had already made his decision on the agreement. Judge Tanner clearly stated that he was only letting the agreement in to show discrimination as he did in the Cassino case. Judge Tanner referenced Cassino in my case to support his decision to admit the *November 1, 1985 document* as a "termination of work agreement," which he did in the Cassino case. In addition, he used it to demonstrate discrimination based on the affidavits of my white co-workers that no other order selector had to waive any rights in order to receive the unemployment benefits. Having overseen the Cassino case, Judge Tanner was familiar with the entire case and the Ninth Circuit supported his decision. In addition, Judge Tanner explained to Mr. Whitters that the *November 1, 1985 document* was also admissible under Federal Rule of Evidence 408 (under this rule evidence is

---

[20]   All of the above are part of the trial court's record related to my case that is also located at the Federal Archive Building in Seattle, WA.

permissible in proving a witness's bias or prejudice). Judge Tanner told Mr. Whitters that the Ninth Circuit just recently ruled on a "General Release" of all claims in the *Cassino* case.

Judge Tanner read the two situations that the Ninth Circuit stated arise in at least two materially distinct contexts. The Ninth Circuit states, "The first is in connection with the negotiation and settlement of disputes arising after the termination." Judge Tanner went on to read that the Ninth Circuit states, "In these cases, an employee relinquishes the right to a judicial determination of an ADEA claim in return **for valuable consideration** after having asserted that he or she is a victim of illegal discrimination." Judge Tanner stated, "The *November 1, 1985 document* did not arise after Mr. Stroman left WCG and Mr. Stroman had not asserted any (federal) claim at the time the *November 1, 1985 document* was presented to him by Mr. Mosley, who is not an attorney."

Then Judge Tanner read from the *Cassino* case where the Ninth Circuit talks about the second situation. Judge Tanner read that the Ninth Circuit stated,

> . . . [in the] second situation appearing in ADEA cases, and one more similar to this case, occurs when an employment relationship is terminated and the employer offers a contemporaneous severance pay package in exchange for a release of all potential claims, including claims for discriminatory acts that may have occurred at or before the termination. Such termination agreements are generally made a part of the record in the case and are considered relevant to the circumstance surrounding the alleged discriminatory discharge itself. The termination

agreements, therefore, are probative on the issue of discrimination.[21]

Judge Tanner stated that the second situation is similar to my case:

> Even though Mr. Stroman was not yet terminated from WCG, the time Mr. Stroman terminated his employment with WCG is when WCG offered unemployment benefits in exchange for a release of all potential claims, including claims for discriminatory acts that may have occurred at or before the termination. The termination agreement, therefore, is probative on the issue of discrimination.[22]

I also believe that Judge Tanner knew from my friends' affidavits that when WCG offered the lay-off to all of the full timers none of them had to waive their union recall rights, or any other rights in order to receive the offer of unemployment benefits. Since I had to waive my union recall rights, it would make the *November 1, 1985 document* probative on the issue of discrimination and I could use it in proving WCG's bias towards me. However, without findings from Judge Tanner on this issue, nobody knows exactly if my friends'

---

[21] According to "The Merriam-Webster Dictionary," copyright 1974, contemporaneous is an adjective for contemporary, which means occurring or existing at the same time.

[22] Thus, with the signing of the November 1, 1985 document and the exchange for a release of all potential claims that happened at the same time, therefore, the November 1, 1985 document is probative on the issue of discrimination according to the Ninth Circuit's ruling in Cassino.

affidavits played a part in Judge Tanner's decision that the actions by WCG surrounding this document was discriminatory; the record only shows Judge Tanner believed it was contemporaneous (i.e. meaning that the offer was given at the same time).

After the above explanation by Judge Tanner, Mr. Whitters kept arguing that the *November 1, 1985 document* was a release of all claims by Mr. Stroman.

Judge Tanner stated, "I made my decision and you are just arguing now." The dialogue between Mr. Whitters and Judge Tanner is also part of the trial court record (an example of this dialogue is included in exhibit 12 on pages 8-10).

After two days, the trial was over. I felt good, because Judge Tanner said before leaving the bench on the last day of trial, "I have not made my findings yet, but I believe Mr. Stroman."

Based on my testimony and the testimony of my witnesses, along with the evidence I submitted during my trial **on April 20, 1988**, Judge Tanner made his decision that I was a victim of intentional racial employment discrimination and constructively discharged. He put his reasons for this decision in three pages of "written findings and conclusion of law" according to Federal Civil Procedure Rule 52 and federal case law. On page three, under Conclusions of Law, Judge Tanner states,

> The denial of training of the plaintiff by the defendant was the result of intentional racial discrimination against the plaintiff by the defendant . . . . The plaintiff was constructively discharged because of the actions and conduct of the defendant herein.

Next Judge Tanner, states in paragraph six,

> The plaintiff is entitled to monetary damages for back pay
> and benefits dating from August 5, 1985, in an amount
> of $101,372.48 . . . . [And] The plaintiff is entitled to front
> pay for five years from the date of judgment due to the
> corporate hostility toward the plaintiff, in the amount of
> $190,073.40.

In total Judge Tanner awarded me, $291,445.88 plus interest (**see exhibit 10**). Judge Tanner did not award me damages against WCG for my state claims (as he had in the *Cassino* case) even though those claims were part of the complaint that McGavick filed for me in federal court.

I believe I was the first individual to win a racial employment discrimination case before Judge Tanner, because during my research I could not find another case where an individual had won a case of racial employment discrimination in a federal district court in the State of Washington. I also believe that I was the first individual to win a racial employment discrimination case after receiving right to sue letters from the EEOC, without the involvement of the EEOC, or the WSHRC during the initial investigation stages when my complaints were filed with them under the 1964 Civil Rights Act.

EXHIBIT #7

ORIGINAL

Honorable Jack E. Tanner

IN THE UNITED STATES DISTRICT COURT FOR THE
WESTERN DISTRICT OF WASHINGTON AT TACOMA

GRADY M. STROMAN,

Plaintiff,

v.

WEST COAST GROCERY COMPANY,

Defendant.

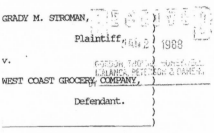

No. C86-528T

PLAINTIFF'S MEMORANDUM IN
OPPOSITION TO
DEFENDANT'S MOTION FOR RECONSI-
DERATION OF DEFENDANT'S MOTION
FOR SUMMARY JUDGMENT

Noted for Motion Docket: 1/29/88

I. STATEMENT OF THE CASE

Defendant's original Motion for Summary Judgment was Denied by this court on
July 2, 1987. Defendant filed a Motion for Reconsideration which was scheduled
for oral argument on August 7, 1987. That motion was postponed when Plaintiff
substituted counsel upon approval of the court. Defendant renewed its Motion for
Reconsideration, now noted for January 29, 1988.

Plaintiff's arguments in opposition to Defendant's motion are contained in
Plaintiff's Memorandum in Opposition to Defendant's Summary Judgment Motion, dated
June 15, 1987; the Affidavit of Plaintiff in Opposition to Defendant's Motion for
Summary Judgment, dated June 6, 1987; Affidavit of Dan Stevenson in Support of
Plaintiff's Opposition to Defendant's Summary Judgment Motion; Affidavit of Rich
Cieplik in Support of Plaintiff's Opposition to Defendant's Summary Judgment
Motion; and the arguments contained in this memorandum. Copies of these documents
are attached for the court's convenience.

II. ARGUMENT

A. The Defendant's Witness Lacks Veracity

The Affidavits of Willie Mosley that Defendant has produced for the court

J. MICHAEL GALLAGHER
ATTORNEY AT LAW
THE OLD VINECOURT BUILDING
300 VINE STREET SUITE 4
(206) 441-7090

indicate that the economic layoff of the Plaintiff, a full time employee, was
Plaintiff's idea. This is a direct contravention of Plaintiff's testimony, which
indicates that Defendant proposed this idea at a employee meeting. However,
Plaintiff's produced affidavits of Rich Cieplik and Dan Stevenson prove that the
Defendant first proposed the idea of economic layoff for full time employees. It
was not Plaintiff's idea. Plaintiff only took the Defendant up on its offer.

Thus, Willie Mosley did not testify to the truth in his affidavits.

If the affidavits of Mosley lack veracity on the point of the economic layoff,
then his entire testimony must be called into question. His testimony re
Plaintiff's understanding of the waiver's terms and coverage must be discounted,
as well as his testimony re his conversations with the Plaintiff. It then becomes
clear that Plaintiff's claims of fraud and coercion re the settlement agreement
must be given its due weight and accepted as true.

B.   The Defendant was Precluded by Contract From Entering Into an Agreement
     With the Plaintiff re His Employment.

Section 17 of the Agreement By and Between Allied Employers, Inc. and
Warehousemen Union Locals Nos. 117 & 599 and Teamsters Union Locals Nos. 252, 378
& 589 prohibited the Defendant from entering into the type of agreement which the
Defendant says bars Plaintiff's suit:

> The Employer agrees not to enter into any agreement or contract with his
> employees individually or collectively, which in any way conflicts with
> the terms and provisions of this Agreement. Any such agreement shall be
> null and void. (Agreement at page 12)

The Agreement between the Plaintiff and the Defendant in question concerned a
modification of his layoff rights. This modification changed his right to recall
as protected by Section 6 of the Agreement. Thus, it was in conflict with Section
6, and thus the Agreement was null and void, according to Section 17 of the
Agreement.

J. Michael Gallagher
ATTORNEY AT LAW
The Old Vinecourt Building.
300 Vine Street. Suite 4

Therefore, Defendant cannot rely on its agreement with the Plaintiff as grounds for its argument that Plaintiff's suit is barred.

III. CONCLUSION

The court must rescind the settlement agreement entered into between the Plaintiff and the Defendant on the grounds of fraud and illegality.

DATED this 25th day of January, 1988.

J. Michael Gallagher
Attorney for the Plaintiff

J. MICHAEL GALLAGHER
ATTORNEY AT LAW
THE OLD VINECOURT BUILDING
300 VINE STREET SUITE 4
(206) 441-7090

EXHIBIT #8

ORIGINAL

IN THE UNITED STATES DISTRICT COURT FOR THE
WESTERN DISTRICT OF WASHINGTON AT TACOMA

GRADY M. STROMAN,　　　　　)
　　　　　　　　　　　　　　　)
　　　　　　Plaintiff,　　　　)　　　No.　C86-528T
　　　　　　　　　　　　　　　)
v.　　　　　　　　　　　　　　)　　　AFFIDAVIT OF RICH CIEPLIK
　　　　　　　　　　　　　　　)　　　IN SUPPORT OF PLAINTIFF'S
WEST COAST GROCERY COMPANY,　)　　　OPPOSITION TO DEFENDANT'S
　　　　　　　　　　　　　　　)　　　SUMMARY JUDGMENT MOTION
　　　　　　Defendant.　　　　)
　　　　　　　　　　　　　　　)
_____)

Rich Cieplik, being first duly sworn, on oath deposes and says:

1. I am eighteen years of age, a citizen of the United States and have knowledge of the facts contained in this affidavit.

2. I am employed at West Coast Grocery and have been since February, 1980. I work in the Grocery Department. I worked with Michael Stroman during that time.

3. On October 29, 1985, I attended a meeting conducted by Willie Mosely. During that meeting, Mosely told a group of 35 employees, both full-time and part-time employees, that the company would be conducting lay-offs. The part-timers would be the first to go. The full-timers weren't going to be laid off unless they wanted to be laid off in order to collect unemployment. Mosely did not include any conditions when making this offer to the full-timers.

4. I called Michael Stroman on October 30, 1985 to tell him about this offer of lay-off for full-timers. I assumed Michael would be interested because it would be a way for him to escape the stress of the job and get paid at the same time.

5. I was surprised when Michael told me that there were conditions to his

J. MICHAEL GALLAGHER
ATTORNEY AT LAW
THE OLD VINECOURT BUILDING
300 VINE STREET, SUITE 4
(206) 441-7090
SEATTLE, WASHINGTON 98121

opting to be laid off. That was not my understanding at Mosely's meeting.

_____
Affiant   DOL# CIEPCPM46268

SUBSCRIBED AND SWORN to before me this _14_ day of _January_, 1987.

_____
Notary Public in and for the
State of Washington, residing at
Tacoma

My commission expires _8/29/91_

J. MICHAEL GALLAGHER
ATTORNEY AT LAW
THE OLD VINECOURT BUILDING
300 VINE STREET, SUITE 4
(206) 441-7000
SEATTLE, WASHINGTON 98121

ORIGINAL

Honorable Jack E. Tanner

IN THE UNITED STATES DISTRICT COURT FOR THE
WESTERN DISTRICT OF WASHINGTON AT TACOMA

GRADY M. STROMAN,

RECEIVED

JAN 25 1988

GORDON, THOMAS, HONEYWELL,
MALANCA, PETERSON & DAHEIM
BY

Plaintiff,

v.

WEST COAST GROCERY COMPANY,

Defendant.

No. C86-528T

AFFIDAVIT OF DAN STEVENSON
IN SUPPORT OF PLAINTIFF'S
OPPOSITION TO DEFENDANT'S
SUMMARY JUDGMENT MOTION

Dan Stevenson, being first duly sworn, on oath deposes and says:

1. I am eighteen years of age, a citizen of the United States and have knowledge of the facts contained in this affidavit.

2. I am employed at West Coast Grocery and have been since February, 1980. I work in the Grocery Department. I worked with Michael Stroman during that time.

3. On October 29, 1985, I attended a meeting conducted by Willie Mosely. During that meeting, Mosely told a group of 35 employees, both full-time and part-time employees, that the company would be conducting lay-offs. The part-timers would be the first to go. The full-timers weren't going to be laid off unless they wanted to be laid off in order to collect unemployment. Mosely did not include any conditions when making this offer to the full-timers.

4. I called Michael Stroman on October 30, 1985 to tell him about this offer of lay-off for full-timers. I assumed Michael would be interested because it would be a way for him to escape the stress of the job and get paid at the same time.

5. I was surprised when Michael told me that there were conditions to his

J. MICHAEL GALLAGHER
ATTORNEY AT LAW
THE OLD VINECOURT BUILDING
300 VINE STREET, SUITE 4
(206) 441-7090
SEATTLE, WASHINGTON 98121

opting to be laid off. That was not my understanding at Mosely's meeting.

(signature)

Affiant

SUBSCRIBED AND SWORN to before me this _30_ day of _Oct._ , 1987.

(signature)

Notary Public in and for the
State of Washington, residing at
Seattle

My commission expires _10/30/87_

J. MICHAEL GALLAGHER

ATTORNEY AT LAW

THE OLD VINECOURT BUILDING
300 VINE STREET, SUITE 4
(206) 441-7090
SEATTLE, WASHINGTON 98121

EXHIBIT #9

IN THE UNITED STATES DISTRICT COURT
FOR THE WESTERN DISTRICT OF WASHINGTON
AT TACOMA

GRADY M. STROMAN,   )

                   Plaintiff,   )   NO. C86-528T

         -vs-   )

WEST COAST GROCERY COMPANY,   )   ORDER

                 Defendant.   )

THIS MATTER comes on before the above-entitled Court upon Defendant's
Motion for Reconsideration of Defendant's Motion for Summary Judgment.

Having considered the entirety of the records and file herein, it is now

ORDERED that Defendant's Motion is DENIED.

The clerk of the court is instructed to send uncertified copies of this order
to all counsel of record.

DATED this _____9____ day of February, 1988.

UNITED STATES DISTRICT JUDGE

EXHIBIT #10

IN THE UNITED STATES DISTRICT COURT
FOR THE WESTERN DISTRICT OF WASHINGTON
AT TACOMA

GRADY M. STROMAN,	)	
Plaintiff,	)	NO. C86-528T
-vs-	)	
WEST COAST GROCERY COMPANY,	)	FINDINGS OF FACT
		AND
Defendant.	)	CONCLUSIONS OF LAW

THIS MATTER coming on for trial before the above-named court, sitting without a jury. Plaintiff appeared through his attorney of record, J. Michael Gallagher. Defendant appeared through its attorney, Timothy J. Whitters.

The court having taken testimony from both parties and having received exhibits from both parties and having listened to argument of counsel and being fully informed in the premises now makes the following:

FINDINGS OF FACT

1. Section "Admitted Facts" of the Amended Joint Pretrial Order dated July 1987, to which the parties have agreed and have admitted as facts are herein incorporated by reference as if fully set forth.

2. Plaintiff is a black male.

3. Before commencing employment at West Coast Grocery, plaintiff had been a corporal and a transportation specialist in the United States Army.

4. During the course of his employment at West Coast Grocery, the plaintiff made numerous and repeated efforts to acquire training for a supervisor's position.

-1-

5.   Defendant had no objective criteria to determine eligibility for training. Any criteria used by management to determine the qualifications of a prospective trainee were subjective and unknown to the general employees of the company, including the plaintiff.   Defendant had no written policy regarding the prerequisites and qualifications for training of employees for supervisory positions.

6.   Plaintiff never was allowed to receive the training in the scheduling office and without the training plaintiff would never have been considered for promotion by the defendant.

7.   There is no correlation between the job of order selector, which plaintiff held, and supervisor. An order selector is a muscle job, loading and pushing pallets of groceries. A supervisor pushes paper.

8.   The plaintiff inquired of Dave Hamlin, operations manager for the defendant, what he needed to do to get the supervisor's training. Hamlin told the plaintiff to read the book, "Up From Slavery", by Booker T. Washington. Plaintiff read the book.

9.   Passages from "Up From Slavery" state that "Negroes must work four times harder than whites" to get ahead, and that other races must conform to the white man's world in order to coexist.

10.   Plaintiff had one community college degree when he commenced employment at West Coast Grocery. While at West Coast Grocery, the Plaintiff acquired another business management-related community college degree.

11.   Because of his race, the plaintiff found the working conditions of the defendant intolerable, thereby causing him to suffer stress on the job, and forcing him to take a unpaid medical leave in August 1985.

12.   That because of defendant's discriminatory conduct, plaintiff suffered economic damages.

The foregoing is based upon a preponderance of the more credible evidence herein.

From the foregoing Findings of Fact, the court now makes the following

CONCLUSIONS OF LAW

1. The court has jurisdiction over the parties and the subject matter of this action pursuant to 42 U.S.C. $2000e, et.seq.

2. Job training is a "term and condition" of employment.

3. The defendant failed to articulate a legitimate, nondiscriminatory business reason for not training the plaintiff and could not point to any objective assessments or criteria to support its decision that plaintiff was not qualified for training.

4. The denial of training of the plaintiff by the defendant was the result of intentional racial discrimination against the plaintiff by the defendant.

5. The plaintiff was constructively discharged because of the actions and conduct of the defendant herein.

6. The plaintiff is entitled to monetary damages for back pay and benefits dating from August 5, 1985, in an amount of $101,372.48.

7. The plaintiff is entitled to front pay for five years from the date of judgment due to the corporate hostility toward the plaintiff, in the amount of $190,073.40.

8. The plaintiff is entitled to his costs and a reasonable attorney's fee for the prosecution of this action.

DATED at Tacoma, Washington, this 20ᵗʰ day of April, 1988.

_____
UNITED STATES DISTRICT JUDGE

-3-

Chapter Thirteen

Events leading up to WCG's Appeal to the 9th Circuit

Based on the ruling by Judge Tanner in my favor, on April 22, 1988, the Tacoma News Tribune printed an article written by Stuart Eskenazi entitled, "Spanaway man wins $291,000 in bias lawsuit." He stated that I was a victim of racial employment discrimination. In that newspaper article, WCG's lead attorney, Timothy Whitters did not mention the *November 1, 1985 document*, nor did he adhere to the agreement, which states that WCG will limit information shared about me to only my date of hire, rate of pay, journeyman status, and they will clear my record. He tried to justify the actions of WCG by stating that I "wasn't a very good worker" and that I "was notorious for turning disagreement into confrontation."

Timothy Whitters made these comments to the news reporter, because he knew that Judge Tanner had ruled that the *November 1, 1985 document* was not valid during the trial. I believe Mr. Whitters knew that part of Judge Tanner's decision was because the *November 1, 1985 document* modified my layoff rights, which meant the document was invalid under the union contract. Based on Judge Tanner's statement during the trial, and the terms under the union contract, Mr. Whitters made these claims to the press to try to save face for the company. I believe this has to be the only reason why Mr. Whitters made these negative comments about me to the newspaper, even though Mr. Whitters and WCG could not convince Judge Tanner. If WCG was somehow planning to appeal the validity of the *November 1, 1985 document* to the Ninth Circuit Court of Appeals then Mr. Whitters should have known that he was limited to only giving out my date of hire, rate of pay, and journeyman status to the newspaper, based on term #3 of the document. Mr. Whitters' statements to the press thus violated the terms of the document, which illustrates that Mr. Whitters may have accepted that the document was invalid, based on Judge Tanner's analysis. Regardless of whether or not Mr. Whitters still believed the document was valid, he violated the terms of the *November 1, 1985 document* when he provided unproven negative comments about my employment history at WCG.

WCG appealed Judge Tanner's April 20, 1988 Findings of Fact and Conclusion of Law that I was a victim of intentional racial employment discrimination and constructive discharge to the Ninth Circuit Court of Appeals. Judge Tanner made no mention of the *November 1, 1985 document* in his Findings of Fact and Conclusion of Law. Because WCG was ordered to pay, WCG had to put the judgment awarded by Judge Tanner in a bond during the appeal process (**see exhibit 11**). With interest, WCG had to put $325,000.00 in a bank account with my name on it.

When WCG filed their appeal brief to the Ninth Circuit Court of Appeals, I remember one part of their brief stated that because of my age I should not be award this large amount of money, since I still had many employment years ahead of me. I remember thinking, "So now WCG's attorney is arguing that I should be treated differently based on my age." In any event, their brief was mostly about how Judge Tanner denied their two attempts to have the *November 1, 1985 document* bar my suit against them. My attorney said, in his brief to the Ninth Circuit Court of Appeals, that it was not proper for WCG to brief an issue that was not part of the trial, or the trial court's record. Furthermore, the appeals court panel could not review Judge Tanner's decision to deny WCG's summary judgment motions according to federal civil procedure rules[23]. In other words, my attorney was saying that after a trial under 28 U.S.C. section 1291, "The courts of appeals shall have

---

[23]   See Federal Rules of Civil Procedure #56.

jurisdiction of appeals from all final decisions of the district courts of the United States . . ."[24] According to Barrow's Law Dictionary, "Findings are decisions of a court on issues of fact or law." Under Federal Rules of Civil Procedure, ". . . an appellate court can only set aside a finding of fact made by a trial judge if determines that the finding is clearly erroneous, i.e., that reasonable men could not possibly make such a finding."

Judge Tanner did not put his decision as to why he denied WCG's summary judgment motions in his finding of fact dated April 20, 1988, which made these summary judgment motions issues not reviewable on appeal by an appellate court panel. The only final decision made by Judge Tanner, supported by his written findings of fact, related to intentional racial discrimination and constructive discharge, which was in front of the Ninth Circuit panel for review under the clearly erroneous standard.

Mr. Whitters was an experienced federal court trial attorney. Furthermore, the big law firm for which he worked had on staff several experienced federal appellate court attorneys, who should have known that WCG could have requested Judge Tanner to make findings on WCG's summary judgment motion, or WCG's reconsideration motion (though Judge Tanner was under no obligation to grant this request). WCG's attorneys knew they were going to appeal Judge Tanner's decision related to his denial of WCG's summary judgment motion and reconsideration motion. In other words, WCG's lead attorney Mr. Whitters had to have known, if the appellate court panel was going to follow the law, that WCG needed Judge Tanner to make findings of fact on at least one of his summary judgment decisions if they wanted the

---

[24]   See 28 U.S.C. section 1291.

summary judgment to be reviewed by the Ninth Circuit. The trial court record establishes that Judge Tanner would not let us litigate the *November 1, 1985 document* during trial, so the appellate court panel had no jurisdiction to review the issue in any other terms than those of the trial court, which stated that it was "probative on the issue of discrimination." In addition, it was "shocking" to me when WCG argued to the Ninth Circuit panel that because Judge Tanner was a member of the black race and perhaps had experienced discrimination, WCG claimed that it was "denied a fair trial" **(see exhibit 12)**.

The Ninth Circuit Court of Appeals three-judge panel heard oral arguments on **January 12, 1989**. During oral arguments at the Ninth Circuit Court of Appeals, Mr. Whitters argued that the Ninth Circuit could rule that I had waived my right to sue WCG, and then the Ninth Circuit would not have to rule on Judge Tanner's written findings of discrimination and constructive discharge. My attorney argued that it was highly improper for the court to hear arguments on an issue that Mr. Whitters knew was denied during WCG's summary judgment motion, which the trial judge did not permit into the trial, and for which there were no findings. My attorney said that Mr. Whitters was trying to persuade the appellate court panel to deny my constitutional right to due process; fully knowing the *November 1, 1985 document* was not litigated between the parties at trial.

In essence, the right thing for the appellate court panel to have done—according to well-established case law and federal civil procedure rules—would have been to remand the issue back to Judge Tanner, and to instruct him to make findings on his denial of WCG's summary judgment motion, or to explain why he was allowing the *November 1, 1985 document* in the trial court record only to show discrimination. According to established case law and federal civil procedure rules, the appellate court panel could only rule on Judge Tanner's findings related to intentional race discrimination and constructive discharge under the *"clearly erroneous standard"* of Federal Civil Procedure Rule 52, since these were the only findings made by Judge Tanner in my case.

When the oral arguments were over, I had faith that these three Ninth Circuit Judges would faithfully, and impartially, perform their duties according to the Constitution and law established by prior Ninth Circuit Court of Appeals rulings and U.S. Supreme Court rulings, pertaining to Federal Civil Procedure Rule 52. My faith, was based on the oath that each federal judge must take prior to becoming a federal judge, which says,

> I do solemnly swear (or affirm) that I will administer justice without respect to persons, and do equal right to the poor and to the rich, that I will faithfully and impartially discharge and perform all the duties incumbent upon me under the Constitution and laws of the United States. So help me God.

EXHIBIT #11

IN THE UNITED STATES DISTRICT COURT
FOR THE WESTERN DISTRICT OF WASHINGTON
AT TACOMA

GRADY M. STROMAN,   )

                  Plaintiff,   )   NO. C86-528T

          -vs-   )

WEST COAST GROCERY COMPANY,   )   ORDER

                Defendant.   )

THIS MATTER Comes on before the above-entitled Court upon Defendant's Motion for Stay of Judgment Pending Appeal.

Having considered the entirety of the records and file herein, it is now

ORDERED that Defendant's Motion for Stay is GRANTED; and it is further

ORDERED that Defendant shall post a supersedeas bond in the amount of $291,445.88, the amount of the trial court judgment and interest, in order to protect plaintiff's interests pending appeal.

The clerk of the court is directed to send uncertified copies of this Order to all parties of record.

DATED this _____7ᵗʰ_____ day of December, 1988.

                            _____
                            UNITED STATES DISTRICT JUDGE

EXHIBIT #12

NINTH CIRCUIT CAUSE NO. 88-3815

IN THE UNITED STATES COURT OF APPEALS
IN AND FOR THE NINTH CIRCUIT

GRADY MICHAEL STROMAN

Plaintiff/Appellee,

vs.

WEST COAST GROCERY COMPANY,
a Washington Corporation,

Defendant/Appellant.

ON APPEAL FROM THE UNITED STATES DISTRICT COURT
FOR THE WESTERN DISTRICT OF WASHINGTON
DISTRICT COURT CAUSE NO. 86-528 JET

BRIEF OF APPELLEE

J. Michael Gallagher
300 Vine Street, Suite 4
Seattle, WA 98121
(206) 441-7090

Appellee's Attorney

II-102-103].

The Agreement by and between Allied Employers, Inc. and
Warehousemen Union et al, effective date 5/1/83 to 4/30/86,
does not recognize that Policy Consultations are forms of
discipline. [Pltf's Ex. 34].

Plaintiff suffered stress on the job due to the
Defendant's treatment of him. He took a medical leave on
August 5, 1985. [RT I-72].

In October, 1985, Plaintiff heard from two of his fellow
employees, Rich Cieplik and Dan Stevenson, that West Coast
Grocery was offering full-time employees the opportunity to
take an economic layoff and thus collect unemployment. The
offer was made by Willie Mosley, Defendant's supervisor,
and was unconditional. [RT I-119; CP 52, 53].

Plaintiff contacted Mosley and stated that he wanted to
take the economic layoff. Mosley told the Plaintiff that he
would have to sign papers giving up his recall rights and
seniority. In return, the Defendant would not contest any
unemployment claims Plaintiff might file. Plaintiff signed
the Agreement dated November 1, 1985. His Title VII claims
were not discussed by him or Mosley. Plaintiff would not
have signed the agreement if he thought the agreement
covered those rights. [CP 20].

Mosely, the only management employee Plaintiff had

- 4 -

contact with re the Agreement, was not aware of what Title

VII was. [RT II-122].

Under the Union Contract, West Coast Grocery agreed not

to enter into any agreement or contract with its

employees/union members, which conflicted with the union

contract. Any such agreement would be null & void. [Pltf's

Ex. 34, at 12].

Plaintiff left employment at West Coast Grocery in

November, 1985. He went to California to attempt to obtain

employment. He was unsuccessful. He collected unemployment

during that time. Since then, he has sporadically held some

different employment positions since leaving West Coast

Grocery. [RT I-32; 129].

III. ARGUMENT

A. The November 1, 1985 Agreement Between Appellant
    and Appellee Constitute a Termination Agreement and
    Not a Settlement Agreement. Thus, the Trial Court
    Did Not Err in Refusing to Dismiss Appellee's
    Claim.

Under common law, rights may be released provided that

the releasor has knowledge of those rights and intends to

release them, Texas Instruments v. Branch Motor Express Co.,

308 F.Supp. 1228 (D.Mass) aff'd 432 F.2d 564 (1st Cir.

1970), and further provided that the release is supported by

valuable consideration. Harmon v. Adams, 120 U.S. 363

- 5 -

(1886). Crucial to the construction of the settlement
agreement is the intent of the parties. Worthy v. McKesson
Corporation, 756 F.2d 1370 (8th Cir. 1985). Intent is a
question of fact. E.G. Pullman-Standard v. Swint, 456 U.S.
273, 288, 72 L.Ed.2d 66 (1982).

Under Title VII, claims arising from "acts or practices
that antedate the execution of the release" may be waived,
provided that the release is supported by valuable
consideration and is "executed voluntarily and with adequate
knowledge." U.S. v. Allegheny-Ludlum Industries, 517 F.2d
826 (5th Cir. 1975), cert.den. 425 U.S. 944 (1976).

However, most importantly, releases "cannot be examined
in a vacuum. A waiver of federal remedial right is not to
be lightly inferred." Watkins v. Scott Paper Co., 530 F.2d
1159 (5th Cir. 1976).

The Appellant would have this court examine the November
1, 1985 Agreement in a vacuum and ignore the fact that the
Appellee did not have an understanding of what the West
Coast Grocery had him sign. [RT I-120].

First, the proposal of an economic layoff was made to
all employees while Stroman was on sick leave without pay,
and not just to Plaintiff as the Appellant stated in its
brief (see, Appellant's Opening Brief, page 18). Plaintiff
was notified of this offer by communications with fellow

- 6 -

employees. [RT I-119; CP 52, 53]. Plaintiff then contacted Willie Mosley, a supervisor, and told him that he was interested in taking the layoff. [CP 17 & 20]. Mosley told him that he would have to come in to sign some papers. [CP 17 & 20]. When Plaintiff was presented with the Agreement and it was explained to him that once he signed the Agreement, he would have no recall rights. [CP 20]. Plaintiff even told Mosley that the Agreement was not affecting his discrimination suits. Mosley agreed with him that it would not. [CP 20].

There was no evidence presented that any other employee was required to sign such an agreement before being placed on an economic layoff. In addition, Plaintiff was on sick leave without pay due to the stress he suffered because of the discrimination at Defendant's business. [RT I-72]). Plaintiff saw the economic layoff as a means to collect unemployment while he sought another job and obtained relief from the discriminatory environment at West Coast Grocery's business. [RT I-72]. The fact that the West Coast Grocery required Plaintiff to sign an agreement to obtain conditionally what it had offered to other employees unconditionally is itself evidence of discrimination.

> Such communications [release agreements] may also tend to be coercive rather than conciliatory. Thus, courts have observed that while an attempt to

- 7 -

mitigate the harshness of a decision to terminate
an employee may be commendable, "courts should not
allow employers to compromise the underlying
policies of the [law] by taking advantage of a
superior bargaining position or by overreaching."
[citations ommitted] "The remedial goals of the
[law] cannot be circumvented by an employer's
coercive practices no matter how subtle the form."
[Citations omitted]

R. Silberman & C. Bolick, The EEOC's Proposed Rule on
Releases of Claims Under the ADEA, 37 Lab.L.J. 195, 195-96
(1986).

The trial court relied on the holding in Cassino v.

Reichhold Chemical, Inc., 817 F.2d 1338 (9th Cir. 1987),

cert.den. 108 S.Ct. 785 (1988) in considering the November

1, 1985 Agreement. The trial court had every right,

according to Cassino, to consider the Agreement as evidence

of intent to discriminate. The court never ruled as a

matter of law that the Agreement could not be considered as

evidence of a release. It just expressed its opinion that

the facts of the Agreement did not warrant its acceptance as

a release.

> MR. WHITTERS: ...And that, in fact, Mr.
> Stroman himself admits that when he looked at it
> [Agreement], he said, I don't know about this last
> one, Willy—so that he was clearly focusing on the
> elements of this release. And even Mr. Stroman
> will testify he understood this release to mean
> that: a) he would have no more seniority; and b)
> he would have no right to recall. In other words,
> he would lose his job by signing that release. And
> he did voluntarily sign the release, and that is
> evidence before this Court, so—
>
> THE COURT: Of what?

- 8 -

MR. WHITTERS: Evidence of waiver and release of the company of the claims.

THE COURT: Well, you're talking about release of claims under Title 7. There's nothing in that release that I can see that refers to Title 7.

MR. WHITTERS: No, it doesn't.

THE COURT: Well?

MR. WHITTERS: It doesn't have to, I suggest to the Court.

THE COURT: It doesn't what?

MR. WHITTERS: It doesn't have to say Title 7 in it. It says all claims.

THE COURT: It's not going to make it.

. . .

MR. WHITTERS: Well, the only difference from Cassino, it seems to me, Your Honor, is that in that instance the company was attempting to keep it out. It was a scenario in which the employee was offered the release as part of a severance package, and he refused to sign it. In this instance we're trying to bring it in, and the employee did sign it.

THE COURT: Well, if I understand the Cassino case, the Court can consider it among all the circumstances involving this whole claim.

[RT-28-29]

MR. WHITTERS: I just don't understand how this agreement violates Title 7, Your Honor.

THE COURT: I didn't say it did.

MR. WHITTERS: Okay.

[RT-128]

In addition, even at the end of trial during closing

- 9 -

arguments, the court indicated it still had an open mind:

> MR. WHITTERS: Your Honor, I didn't say this in my final argument, but I don't want any implication that I waive it, and I hope no one construes that I have. We still maintain that the agreement of November 1st, '85, was a release agreement.

> THE COURT: I would expect that to be an issue in this case.

Finally, as far as discriminatory intent, it makes no difference under Cassino whether the Agreement was signed or not. What is important is whether the Agreement is evidence of discriminatory intent, and it was.

Further, once the trial court had determined that the Agreement was evidence of discrimination, it was not bound to uphold its terms, even if it was a valid agreement on its face re Title VII. Employment Agreements in violation of Title VII should not be upheld. 42 U.S.C. §2000e-2.

It should also be noted that the Union contract prohibits separate agreements such as the November 1, 1985 Agreement, and if the employer does so contract, then the agreement is null & void. [Pltf's Ex. 34, at 12].

Therefore, the trial court did not commit error when it refused to accept the Defendant's arguments re the November 1, 1985 Agreement and refused to dismiss Stroman's claims.

Appellant also tries to argue that a finding of constructive discharge necessarily assumes that West Coast Grocery's failure to train Appellee was intentional discrimination. [Appellant's Opening Brief, at 34-35]. Again Appellant fails to understand the law of constructive discharge and what happened at trial.

According to the court in Watson v. Nationwide Ins. Co., 823 F.2d 360 (9th Cir. 1987), the plaintiff need not show that the employer subjectively intended to force the employee to resign; he only must show some aggravating factors such as a continuous pattern of discriminatory treatment. Watson also held that the trial court's factual findings should be upheld when the Plaintiff is subjected to incidents of differential treatment over a period of months or years. That is what happened to the Plaintiff in this case.

Other court decisions are instructive in this matter. In Derr v. Gulf Oil Corporation, 796 F.2d 340, 344 (10th Cir. 1986) the court said:

> To the extent that the employer denies a conscious design to force the employee to resign, we note that an employer's subjective intent is irrelevant; the employer must be held to have intended those consequences it could reasonably have foreseen.

(emphasis supplied by the court).

1504, 1512 (1985):

> If the district court's account of the evidence is
> plausible in light of the record viewed in its
> entirety, the court of appeals may not reverse it
> even though convinced that had it been sitting as
> the trier of fact, it would have weighed the
> evidence differently.

Thus, absent evidence of a clear error by the trial court, the Court of Appeals cannot upset the Findings of Fact re constructive discharge because there was sufficient evidence to support it.

Finally, the argument of the Appellant that the trial court did not allow it the opportunity to present evidence is just not supported by the record. See Dave Hamlin's testimony [RT I-188-189, 195-196], Pete Clark's testimony [RT II-90, 96] and Charles Young's testimony [RT II-28-34].

Therefore, the Appellant's arguments re constructive discharge are without merit and the trial court's findings must be upheld.

D. <u>There Was Evidence of Appellee's Mitigation
Efforts, and to the Extent There Wasn't, Appellant
Waived its Right to Produce Contrary Evidence.</u>

<u>Cassino v. Reichhold Chemical, Inc.</u>, 817 F.2d 1338 (9th Cir. 1987), cert. den. 108 S.Ct. 785 (1988), held that a plaintiff must attempt to mitigate damages by exercising reasonable care and diligence in seeking reemployment after

in its pretrial order [CP **], the court was under no
obligation to entertain such evidence. The departure from
or adherence to the pretrial order is a matter peculiarly
within the discretion of the trial judge. Beissel v.
Pittsburgh and Lake Erie R.Co., 801 F.2d 143, cert.den. 107
S.Ct. 1296 (3rd Cir. 1986).

Finally, the Defendant waived mitigation by objection to
Plaintiff's evidence on that point and by failing to show
that there were suitable positions available and that the
Plaintiff had failed to use reasonable care in seeking
them. [RT 192-194].

Thus, the Appellant failed to carry its burden under
Cassino.

Therefore, the trial court did not err because it was
Appellant who failed to augment the record with the
appropriate evidence.

E.   The Front Pay Award Was Appropriate in This Case.

Awards of front pay in Title VII suits are appropriate
when it is impossible to reinstate plaintiff or when it
would be inappropriate due to excessive hostility or
antagonism between the parties. Thorne v. City of Segundo,
802 F.2d 1131 (9th Cir. 1986).

Further, the court in Fadhl v. City & County of San
Francisco, 741 F.2d 1163 (9th Cir. 1984), said an award of

front pay is made in lieu of reinstatement when the
antagonism between employer and employee is so great that
reinstatement is not appropriate.

In this case, evidence of West Coast Grocery's hostility
toward the Plaintiff is rampant. See testimony of Hamlin
[RT II-13] and Clark [RT II-89-101]. It should be obvious
that reinstatement would not be appropriate. Thus, the
court ordered five years of front pay, presumably due to the
fact that the Plaintiff had been largely unsuccessful in
obtaining employment since his separation from West Coast
Grocery.

According to the court in Fitzgerald v. Sirloin
Stockade, Inc., 624 F.2d 945 (10th Cir. 1980), a reviewing
court is reluctant to interfere with the trial court's
design of a remedy for employment discrimination. Also,
Falcon v. GTE of Southwest, 626 F.2d 369 (5th Cir. 1980).

The Fitzgerald court also found that the trial court has
broad discretion in fashioning relief to achieve the broad
purpose of eliminating the effects of discriminatory
employment practices and in restoring the subject of
employment discrimination to the position that he or she
would have likely enjoyed had it not been for the
discrimination. In the Fitzgerald case, five years of front
pay was upheld without any discount to present value. See
also, Gross v. Exxon Office Sys. Co., supra, at 888, which

- 28 -

held that the choice of awarding front pay in lieu of reinstatement in a Title VII case rests in the sound discretion of the trial court.

There is no evidence that West Coast Grocery would have wanted Plaintiff's return to employment. There is also much evidence of discrimination, intent, and hostility toward the Plaintiff. Further, it is likely to assume that without the discrimination against the Plaintiff, Plaintiff would still be employed at the West Coast Grocery, probably in a position with more pay than an order selector. At present, Plaintiff's job prospect outlook is bleak.

Therefore, the trial court did not err in awarding five years of front pay.

F. The Trial Court Acted Fair and Unbiased During the Proceedings; Appellant Was not Denied a Fair Trial.

The Appellant seeks reversal of the trial court's decision on the grounds that 1. it would not allow the admission of certain evidence, which would have been either cumulative or irrelevant; 2. it cross-examined witnesses; and 3. that it was biased because the trial judge was a member of the black race and perhaps had experienced discrimination such that he was predisposed and could not fairly judge the case. All of these accusations against the trial judge are misplaced, inappropriate and incorrect.

According to Clady v. County of Los Angeles, 770 F.2d 1421 (9th Cir. 1985), evidentiary rulings are not reversible absent clear abuse of discretion. The evidence that Defendant sought to introduce re Plaintiff's work performance, and which were disallowed by the court (see Appellant's Opening Brief, at 42), had already come into evidence through prior testimony. [RT II-90, -96, -111, -163]. Thus, it was cumulative and properly excluded.

Further, according to Crandall v. United States, 703 F.2d 74 (4th Cir. 1983), the trial judge is entitled to propound questions pertinent to factual issues which require clarification; he may intercede because of apparent inadequacy of examination or cross examination by counsel, or to draw more information from relevant witnesses or experts who are inarticulate or less than candid. This is exactly what the trial court did when it questioned the defense witnesses. It acted properly. See also, N.L.R.B. v. Central Press of California, 527 F.2d 1156 (9th Cir. 1975), where neither the administrative law judge's determinations of credibility adverse to the employer nor his questions to witnesses supported the employer's allegations of judicial bias in the proceeding.

Finally, the Appellant alleges that an interchange with Defense counsel re the trial judge's service in the Army as a corporal in a Jim Crow regiment was indicative of the judge's predisposition towards racial discrimination matters. The Appellant would have the trial judge disqualified and his decision reversed due to his life experiences. This is preposterous and contrary to the law.

In U.S. v. Peltier, 529 F.Supp. 549 (C.D.CA. 1982), the trial court's alleged comment at side bar: "I have lived and gone to school with those kind of people all my life so I know those kind of people," was so unspecific that it had no meaning within the context of a motion for recusal filed by the defendant in a criminal case.

In Tafero v. Wainwright, 796 F.2d 1314, reh.den. 807 F.2d 999, cert,den. 107 S.Ct 3277 (11th Cir. 1986), the fact that the trial judge in a trial for the murder of a police officer had alllegedly attended and had emotional reaction at one victim's funeral did not establish personal bias or prejudice that constituted bias.

The court in U.S. v. Reeves, 782 F.2d 1323, cert.den. 107 S.Ct. 136 (5th Cir. 1986)said to justify the disqualification of a judge, alleged bias and prejudice must stem from an extrajudicial source and result in an opinion on the merits on some basis other than what the judge learned during the presentation of the case.

Another court, U.S. v. Cohen, 644 F.Supp. 113 (E.D.

Mich. 1986), held that intemperate statements or bias claimed to derive from a judge's background do not require disqualification.

All of the above authority shows that the trial judge's conduct was not improper and that his background is not grounds for recusal from the case.

IV. CONCLUSION

Appellee respectfully suggests that the Appellant has failed to show any reason why the trial court decision should be reversed and/or remanded. Therefore, Appellee asks that this court AFFIRM the entire decision of the trial court and award him his attorney's fees pursuant to 42 U.S.C. §2000e-5(k).

Respectfully submitted this 26th day of October, 1988.

J. Michael Gallagher
Appellee's Attorney

Chapter Fourteen

While waiting for the 9th Circuit Court of Appeals Ruling

While I was waiting for the Ninth Circuit ruling, in **April 1989**, I did some research on Judge Tanner to find out more about him. I did this because I wanted to know why it seemed to me that so many people (mainly non-black individuals) spoke negatively about his rulings and about him as a federal judge. During my research, I learned that Judge Tanner grew up in Tacoma; that he was a star athlete while he was in high school in the Tacoma area; and after graduating from high school; he enlisted in the U.S. Army during World War II. He served in the Pacific in a segregated unit. In other words, his military unit consisted of all black enlistment men and all white officers. Up until 1948, the military adhered to "Jim Crow Laws" (based in part on the belief of "white supremacy"). Thus, only white officers could command fighting units and were bestowed roles of leadership. I can remember Judge Tanner stating during my trial that he was in the "Jim Crow Army," and that while he was in the Army, he saw discrimination firsthand and these experiences are part of his life.

From my research, I found out that once his enlistment was done he came back to Tacoma and worked as a longshoreman on the docks in Tacoma. He also went to school at the College of Puget Sound, and later went to the University of Washington Law School. While in law school, he joined the NAACP and later served as regional director from 1957-1965. He also marched in Mississippi during the Civil Rights movement, and led protest marches in the early 60's in Kennewick, Washington. I read that in 1963, he conferred with President Kennedy in the White House on race relations following the assassination of Medgar Evers. In 1978, President Carter appointed Tanner to the federal district court; Tanner was the first black federal judge in the State of Washington. In 1980, Tanner ruled that the Washington State prison at Walla Walla had violated the "cruel and unusual punishment" clause of the Eighth Amendment, and in 1983, he made a landmark ruling on "comparable worth" which pertains to economic rights for women[25].

The more I learned about Judge Tanner, the more I started to realize that the majority of people who diminished his accomplishments and/or complained about his rulings were those who felt threatened and/or stood to lose from a just and equitable application of the law. I came to the conclusion that because he was an educated, strong, out-spoken black man, who was not afraid to express his opinion, or rule against the status quo when the evidence proves/shows the status quo is wrong according to the law, were probably some of the reasons why so many non-black individuals had problems with his appointment, his actions, and his rulings as a federal judge.

On **May 13, 1989**, The Morning News Tribune printed an article about the Washington Human Rights Commission (WSHRC) entitled, "Plagued agency unveils organization proposal." The author, Leslie Brown summarized an investigation by the state Office of Financial Management that "was highly critical" of the WSHRC. The article stated,

> The organization [is] plagued by poor management, low morale, internal distrust and inefficient case management. As a result of these problems, the agency has fallen further and further behind in processing discrimination cases.

---

[25] I found this information about Judge Jack Tanner at The Tacoma Public Library.

A short time after this newspaper article was published, the public was asked to air complaints about the WSHRC and how cases of racial discrimination had been handled. Mr. Lee and I, among others, testified at this public hearing at the Port of Seattle. Mr. Lee testified, based on his interactions with several individuals who filed complaints with the WSHRC under Washington State Law (RCW 49.60), that there is a lack of enforcement of this Washington State Law, which prohibits employment discrimination. I testified that the WSHRC never investigated the racial employment discrimination complaints I filed against WCG. Additionally, I testified that a WSHRC employee tried to deny my third right to sue letter against a major corporation in Tacoma claiming that I had "waived my right to sue this corporation" based only on the word of corporate agents. I also testified that after receiving my first two right to sue letters, I filed them in federal court and I later proved my allegations of intentional racial discrimination using the same evidence and witnesses that I had given the WSHRC.

After the public hearing, on **June 23, 1989**, the Seattle Times published an article written by the Associate Press entitled "Detractor replaces Human Rights official," which announced that the Commissioner of the WSHRC was removed from his position as the Director of the WSHRC.

After the public hearing by the WSHRC, based on the ruling from Judge Tanner in my case, and the newspaper articles about the WSHRC, Mr. Lee and I decided that we would hold a seminar about how to establish a prima facie case before filing an allegation of racial employment discrimination under the 1964 Civil Rights Act with the EEOC or the WSHRC. I asked Dr. Maxine Mimms at Evergreen State College if I could reserve a classroom to hold a seminar on Title VII of the 1964 Civil Rights Act. After leaving

WCG, I sought a bachelor degree at Evergreen and met Dr. Mimms when I was an undergraduate student. Dr. Mimms was the Dean of the campus in the Tacoma Hilltop area, which is a predominantly black community. She was strongly committed to, and deeply involved in improving the black community through education. Dr. Mimms agreed to let Mr. Lee and me use one of the classrooms at Evergreen to hold our seminar.

During the same conversation, Dr. Mimms told me that she read about the judgment awarded to me in the newspaper and we talked about the trial. I got the impression that Dr. Mimms admired me for standing up to the discrimination at WCG. However, once I told her about the appeal, she said, "The Ninth Circuit is not going to let a young black man like you receive the judgment by Judge Tanner." She said that I should take the settlement offer that WCG had on the table, which was $100,000.00 (but I would only receive $70,000.00 because my attorney would get one third of the settlement amount).

When Dr. Mimms said that the Ninth Circuit Court of Appeals was not going to let Judge Tanner's verdict stand because I was a young black man, it reminded me of similar things McGavick had said. I also thought to myself that Dr. Mimms was saying that I could not win on the merits and the truth of my case. My perspective at this time was that she was saying I could only lose because I am a young black man. I then said,

If I took the settlement offer then no one would know how the Ninth Circuit Court of Appeals would act when a young black individual wins a major racial employment discrimination case. No one would know about the discrimination at WCG because I would have to agree that

WCG did nothing wrong. If I did this, then my employment
discrimination complaints were for money only.

With that, my conversation with Dr. Mimms ended.

Sure, I wanted the money that WCG had to put into the bank
account for me, and since the ruling had been in my favor, WCG
would have to pay my attorney for me, which meant that all of the
money in the bank account would have been mine. Additionally, I
wanted Judge Tanner's ruling so that it would show others that a
young black individual could win a Title VII case in federal court
in the State of Washington. Furthermore, since I have not found
a case where a black individual won in federal court for racial
employment discrimination in the State of Washington, I wanted
to be the first one without the help of the EEOC or the WSHRC.

Chapter Fifteen

The 9th Circuit ruling in Stroman v. West Coast Grocery

On **August 31, 1989**, it turned out that McGavick and Dr. Mimms knew what they were talking about. Two of the judges on the three-judge panel, decided to overturn Judge Tanner's summary judgment decision not to grant WCG's summary motions[26]. Thus, in essence saying that the trial should have never happened, even though the evidence shows there were no findings of fact made by Judge Tanner on WCG's summary judgment motions related to the *November 1, 1985 document* (**see exhibit 13**, *Stroman v. West Coast Grocery,* 884 F.2d 458)[27].

At the oral arguments, I remember Mr. Whitters telling the panel to only rule on the issue of the *November 1, 1985 document*, because then they would not have to rule on Judge Tanner's findings of fact related to intentional race discrimination and constructive discharge against WCG. Mr. Whitters instructed the panel to do this, knowing Judge Tanner did not allow WCG or me to litigate the issue of a waiver at trial, and did not let either side introduce any evidence on the waiver issue in the trial court record/transcripts. In any event, two of the judges on the panel did exactly this.

When my attorney told me that Judge Tanner's ruling was reversed based on the *November 1, 1985 document* by these two judges, I was totally surprised and upset. I could not figure out how the Ninth Circuit believed I waived my racial employment discrimination complaints filed under Title VII when I received a

---

[26] Not Judge Tanner's Findings of Facts and Conclusion of Law pertaining to his ruling of intentional racial employment discrimination and constructive discharge against WCG.

[27] Remember Judge Tanner never made any findings pertaining to WCG's summary judgment motion relating to me waiving my employment discrimination complaints or my right to sue WCG under Title VII.

right to sue letter for each complaint according to the guidelines established by the EEOC. I went to my attorney's office to get a copy of the ruling so that I could read it, and afterwards I took it over to Mr. Lee's house so that he could read it as well. After he read it, he could not believe these two judges stated that Judge Tanner made findings on the *November 1, 1985 document* (because he did not) and Mr. Lee became very upset.

Afterwards I called my attorney to ask what would be the next step. He stated, "I tried to tell you to take the settlement offer of the One Hundred Thousand Dollars ($100,000.00) made by WCG. Now your case is worth nothing." Reluctantly, he told me that we could file a reconsideration motion and an appeal to the whole Ninth Circuit, but he would have to think about it.

During this time, I went to the law library and read all of the cases that were cited by these two appellate judges in their ruling. In addition, I consulted with lawyers, and based on these cases, I will show that:

(1) An appellate court panel can only review decisions by a district court judge when there are findings of fact on those decisions specifically made by that district court judge.

(2) When a Ninth Circuit panel finds evidence on the district court record causing them to disagree with a district court's findings, the panel cannot make contrary findings, but rather must remand the case back to district court for reconsideration. [28]

(3) Before an appellate panel can review a contract or agreement dispute between the parties, **(a)** the district court

---

[28] It would still be the same if this evidence was found on the district court trial court record/transcripts.

judge must make findings of fact on this issue, and **(b)** those findings of fact need to state whether they are based on an analysis of contractual language, or based upon extrinsic evidence of related facts. [29]

(4) The two appellate court judges completely disregarded existing federal guidelines for the validity of a Title VII release of claims, and their ruling went on to diminish the established guidelines from six criteria to two for race discrimination plaintiffs.

(5) The Ninth Circuit ruled in a case before mine that a termination agreement could be used to show discrimination.

(6) These two appellate court judges in my case perpetrated fabrications to set aside the district court judge's findings of fact related to intentional racial employment discrimination.

(7) The two appellate court judges in my case acted outside their judicial jurisdiction, making them trespassers of the law.

(8) I believe the ruling by these two appellate court judges in my case was racially motivated.

1) An appellate court panel can only review decisions by a district court judge when there are findings of fact on those decisions specifically made by that district court judge.

---

[29] An analysis of the contractual language is the wording of the document itself, and according to "The Free Dictionary" extrinsic evidence . . . not furnished by the document in and of itself but is derived from external sources . . . it is not within a contract but, rather, is oral and outside the instrument.

I have already proven by **exhibit 10** that the only findings of fact in my case pertain to the district court judge's decision that I was a victim of intentional racial discrimination and constructive discharge. By law, if there are no findings of fact by a district court judge related to a specific issue after a trial between the parties, an appellate court panel cannot review that issue. In addition, if the district court judge refused to allow the parties to introduce evidence on an issue in the trial court record/transcripts, an appellate court panel has no jurisdiction to hear arguments on that issue during oral arguments, or to make a decision on that issue after oral arguments. If the district court judge granted summary judgment to one of the parties essentially dismissing the case, then the district court judge would make findings of fact supporting his/her decision. Afterwards, an appellate court would have jurisdiction to review those findings of fact.

By law, a federal appellate court can make decisions on a district court judge's findings of fact if the district court judge has made a legal error. In addition, under Federal Civil Procedure Rule 52, once a district court judge makes findings of fact on issues after a trial, or after a summary judgment motion, an appellate court cannot reverse those findings unless those findings of fact were clearly erroneous[30]. Most of all, an appellate court cannot dismiss the case, but rather the panel must remand the case back to the district court judge to reconsider his/her findings of fact if the appellate court has issues with the district court judge's findings of fact. As I have stated throughout this story, the federal district court judge in my case did not make any findings of fact on the *November 1, 1985 document* after the federal district court judge

---

[30] The clearly erroneous standard means that a reasonable person would not have come to the same conclusion.

denied WCG's summary judgment motions. [31] When the district court judge did incorporate the *November 1, 1985 document* into the trial court record/transcripts, he stated that he was letting the document in to show discrimination.

Now, according to federal law that is cited in the U.S. Supreme Court ruling in *Alexander v. Gardner-Denver Co.*, 415 U.S. 36, 94 S. Cit. 1011, 39 L.Ed2d 147 (1974), the Court held, "That an employee may validly waive claims of discrimination so long as the waiver is made knowingly and willfully." Additionally, in footnote #15 the Court held, "In determining the effectiveness of any such waiver, a court would have to determine at the **outset** that the employee's consent to the settlement was voluntary and knowing"[32] [emphasis mine]. In essence, for an appellate court to review whether an employee under Title VII has waived his/her federal claims of discrimination there must be findings of fact at the "**outset**" by the district court judge stating that the "**employee's consent to the settlement was voluntary and knowing.**"[33] If the district court judge allows the employment discrimination case to go to trial, then the district court judge was not convinced that the employee's consent to a waiver was voluntary and knowing. Federal law states, "It is the district court judge who must first make this determination and not

---

[31]   Remember in my case WCG was the defendant, whose summary judgment motions were denied by the district court judge based on the issue that the November 1, 1985 document was a waiver agreement of Title VII claims, without findings of fact, and afterwards my case went to trial.

[32]   An employee's rights under Title VII may not be waived prospectively.

[33]   These findings of fact would be at the end of a summary judgment motion, if the defendant convinced the trial court judge that the employee's consent to the waiver was voluntary, willful, and knowing.

the appellate courts." Without district court findings of fact regarding consent to a waiver, an appellate court has no legal authority to address this issue.

The two Ninth Circuit cases (*Salmeron v. United States, 724 F.2d 1357, 1361, and Jones v. Taber, 648 F.2d 1201, 1203*) cited by these two federal appellate court judges in my case to support the statement that, "The interpretation and validity of a release of Title VII claims is governed by federal law," **are not Title VII cases.**[34] These cases do not apply to my case, because in both of those cases:

(a) The district court judge made findings of fact in favor of the defendants during their summary judgment motion on the issue of a waiver of federal rights; and

(b) Based on the summary judgment ruling by the district court judge the cases did not go to trial until after the appeal to the Ninth Circuit on the summary judgment motion.

2) *When a Ninth Circuit panel finds evidence on the district court record causing them to disagree with a district court's findings, the panel cannot make contrary findings, but rather must remand the case back to district court for reconsideration.*

An appellate court panel cannot substitute its interpretation of the evidence for that of the trial court judge, such as weighing the strengths, merits and/or credibility of specific pieces of evidence

---

[34] In each of these two cases, there was a signed waiver agreement between the parties and the district court was convinced that a waiver of federal rights was made before the parties went to trial.

(e.g. affidavits, witness testimony, etc.) submitted during a summary judgment motion.

The U.S. Supreme Court ruled in *Inwood Laboratories, Inc., et. Al., v. Ives Laboratories, Inc. Darby Drug Co., Inc., et. al.,* 456 U.S. 844, 102 S.Ct. 2182, 72 L.Ed.2d 606 (1982),

> An appellate court cannot substitute its interpretation of the evidence for that of the trial court simply because the reviewing court might give the fact another construction . . .

In addition, the Court ruled, ". . . The Court of Appeals clearly erred. Determining the weight and credibility of the evidence is the special province of the trier of fact." These two appellate judges, in my case, stated that the district court judge, ". . . permit West Coast's counsel to make an offer of proof incorporating Mosley's affidavit in the trial court record/transcripts." When one looks at trial court record/transcripts it shows that the trial court judge denied every offer of proof by WCG's lead trial attorney pertaining to Mosley's affidavit. This fact is consistence with the trial court judge denying WCG's summary judgment motions where Mosley's affidavits are part of the court's record during the summary judgment motions, but were denied to be part of the trial court record/transcripts by the district court judge. In other words, if the trial court judge believed what Mosley stated in his affidavits then WCG would have won at the summary judgment level. Furthermore, if the trial court judge did incorporate one of Mosley's affidavits in the trial court record/transcripts, as stated by these two appellate court judges, they should have stated where in the trial court record/transcripts this happened. Based only on the Mosley affidavit (that two of the appellate court judges stated was incorporated in the trial court's record—though it was not), they ruled, "We conclude that the record as a whole sufficiently establishes the voluntariness of the agreement." Meanwhile, they knew that there was no oral testimony at trial, or findings of fact on this issue by the district court judge. To me it is obvious that these two appellate court judges did what WCG's lead trial attorney asked them to do, which was for the panel to rule that the *November 1, 1985 document* was an effective waiver of my Title VII claims. Because the district court did not make findings of fact on the waiver issue, these two appellate court judges should have remanded my case back to the district court judge. By law, this is the only way these appellate court judges can revisit why the district court judge denied WCG's summary judgment motions.

For the sake of argument, let us say Mosley's affidavit is part of the trial court record/transcripts. Even if this was true (which it is not) according to the above U.S. Supreme Court ruling the determination on the weight and credibility of the evidence is the special province of the 'trier of fact.'[35] An appellate court panel cannot substitute its interpretation of the evidence for that of the trial court judge, nor put weight and credibility on an affidavit for which the district court judge placed no credibility during WCG's summary judgment motions, meaning the two appellate court judges had no legal jurisdiction to place any weight or credibility on Mosley's affidavit.[36]

---

[35] In this instance, Mosley's affidavit would be evidence.

[36] Remember, after the trial Judge Tanner ruled in his findings of fact that my evidence was more credible, meaning these two appellate court judge can not substitute its opinion on the credibility of Mosley's affidavit over Judge Tanner's ruling in his findings of fact.

3) Before an appellate panel can review a contract or agreement dispute between the parties, (a) the district court judge must make findings of fact on this issue, and (b) those findings of fact need to state whether they are based on an analysis of the contractual language, or based upon extrinsic evidence of related facts.[37]

In two other cases cited by these two appellate judges (*Miller v. Safeco Title Ins. Co.*, 758 F.2d 364, 367-68, 1985, and *Marchese v. Shearson Hayden Stone, Inc.*, 734 F.2d 414, 417, 1984), they talk about a standard of review called "de novo," and how the Ninth Circuit used this review in both of the above cases when the district court judge's findings of fact were based on an analysis of the contractual language and an application of the principles of contract interpretation. In both of these cases the Ninth Circuit stated, "The interpretation of a contract is a mixed question of law and fact."

> In the Miller case, the court states the standard for review is as follows:

> When the district court's decision (findings of fact) is based on an analysis of the contractual language and an application of the principles of contract interpretation, that decision is a matter of law and reviewable de novo. When the inquiry focuses on extrinsic evidence of related facts,

---

[37] Extrinsic evidence is evidence not within the November 1, 1985 document but related to the document (i.e. depositions, affidavits, and exhibits), and an analysis of the contractual language is the wording of the document itself.

however, the trial court's conclusions will not be reversed unless they are clearly erroneous." [emphasis added]

In the Marchese case, the court stated the standard of review is as follows:

If the district court makes factual findings concerning what the parties said and did, they are subject to clearly erroneous review.

In essence, both cases are stating that before an appellate panel can review a contract or agreement dispute between the parties, the district court judge must make findings of fact as to whether those findings of fact were based on an analysis of the contractual language, or based upon extrinsic evidence of related facts.

The two appellate judges stated in my case,

The district court conclusion that the November 1, 1985, agreement did not constitute a release of all claims . . . was based primarily on an analysis of the contract provisions.

They made this statement without any findings of fact from the district court judge surrounding a release of claims. They then stated, in so many words, that they have the jurisdiction to review the district court determination de novo based on the rulings by the Ninth Circuit in *Miller v. Safeco Title Ins. Co,* and *Marchese v. Shearson Hayden Stone, Inc.* Based on the two above cited cases these two appellate court judges had no legal jurisdiction to review this issue because there were no district judge findings of fact on this issue.

4) **These two appellate court judges completely disregarded existing federal guidelines for the validity of a Title VII release of claims, and their ruling went on to diminish the established guidelines from six criteria to two for race discrimination plaintiffs.**

Before the two appellate court judges made their ruling in my case, there already was established case law pertaining to the validity of a Title VII release of claims, upheld and clarified by the Ninth Circuit and other circuit courts. In fact, these two appellate court judges cited *Coventry V. United States Steel Corp.*, 856 F.2d 514, 522 (3rd Cir 1988) which specifically identifies that in determining the validity of a release of Title VII claims, the release must be done so voluntarily, deliberately, and informed. The court in the Coventry's case relied on six criteria set out in *E.E.O.C. v. American Express Publishing Corp.*, 681 F.Supp. 216 (S.D.N.Y. 1988) by that federal district court.

When one also looks at the case law cited by these two appellate court judges, in my case, surrounding the determination of a waiver of Title VII claims they state:

> The determination of whether a waiver of Title VII was voluntary, deliberate, and informed is predicated upon an evaluation of several indicia arising from the circumstances and conditions under which the release was executed." Citing *Coventry v. United States Steel Corp.*, 856 F.2d 514, 522 (3rd Cir 1988).

Now let us look at *Coventry v. United States Steel Corp.*, which involved a knowingly and willingly signed release of federal rights. In this case, the court stated in part,

> . . . in our view, the inquiry into the validity of a release of discrimination claims does not end with the evaluation that would be applied to determine the validity of a contract. In light of the strong policy concerns to eradicate discrimination in employment, a review of the totality of the circumstances, considerate of the particular individual who has executed the release, is also necessary.

In *Coventry*, the court used the ruling in *E.E.O.C. v. American Express Publishing Corp.*, 681 F.Supp. 216 (S.D.N.Y 1988) because that court's rationale was compelling in determining the evaluation of the validity of a waiver ADEA claims. The court held that the, "[d]etermination of whether a release is voluntary depends on":

1) The plaintiff's education and business experience,
2) The amount of the time the plaintiff had possession of or access to the agreement before signing it,
3) The role of plaintiff in deciding the terms of the agreement,
4) The clarity of the agreement,
5) Whether the plaintiff was represented by or consulted with an attorney, and
6) Whether the consideration given in exchange for the waiver exceeds employee benefits to which the employee was already entitled by contract or law.

Since there were no findings of fact by the district court judge, there is no evidence for an appellate court review to show that the district court judge did not use these six compelling criteria. It is obvious that the district court judge, in my case, did not believe that I waived my Title VII claims, since the district court judge let my case proceed to trial after there were two summary judgment motions on this issue by WCG.[38] Besides, it is the district court judge who determines if the waiver was voluntary, using the above criteria at the outset of a trial and not by the appellate court after a trial.

5) The Ninth Circuit ruled in a case before mine that a termination agreement could be used to show discrimination.

From the ruling by these two appellate judges in my case, we know that the district court judge believed that the *November 1, 1985 document* was a termination agreement and it was discriminatory.[39] The district court judge had jurisdiction to use the analysis pertaining to the *November 1, 1985 document* that was used in *Cassino*, related to a termination agreement. As was stated

---

[38] In chapter 18, I will show how the Ninth Circuit quietly reversed the ruling of a federal district court judge who used the criteria set in my case by these two appellate court judges during a summary judgment motion in an ADEA case—*Parker v. U.S. Suzuki Motor Corporation.*

[39] One can conclude that Judge Tanner made his decision that it was a termination agreement after reviewing all of the evidence submitted to him during the summary judgment motions showing I was terminating my employment at the same time WCG was offering a release of all potential claims.

earlier, Judge Tanner oversaw the *Cassino* case even though a jury decided that Cassino was a victim of age discrimination. In that case, the jury made findings of facts and conclusion of law. The Ninth Circuit upheld the discrimination part of those findings of fact, however, remanded the case back to the district court on the monetary award.

The Ninth Circuit ruling in *Cassino v. Reichhold Chemicals, Inc,* 817 F.2d 1338 (1987) pertaining to a termination agreement states under Federal Rule of Evidence 408,

> Such termination agreements are generally made a part of the record in the case and are considered relevant to the circumstances surrounding the alleged discriminatory discharge itself.

Let us compare Cassino and my case. Both Cassino and I filed a complaint with the WSHRC for violation of Title VII of the 1964 Civil Rights Act. In both cases, the employer offered some sort of an agreement. The Ninth Circuit upheld the ruling that Cassino, an age discrimination plaintiff, had not asserted any federal claims since he had not filed a complaint in federal court when the agreement was offered to him. Nevertheless, in my case these two appellate court judges ruled that I, a race discrimination plaintiff, had asserted federal claims knowing that I had not filed a complaint in federal court when WCG offered me the *November 1, 1985 document.* However, Cassino's agreement was over four pages long and drafted by an attorney who specifically cited that he would have to waive his WSHRC complaint and his rights under Title VII.

In my case, the *November 1, 1985 document* was not even a page long, no one knows who drafted the document and the document did not state anything surrounding my WSHRC complaints or rights under Title VII. Cassino, who was a well-experienced sophisticated businessperson, refused to sign his informed agreement. Because the *November 1, 1985 document* did not mention me waiving my WSHRC complaint or rights under Title VII, but only stated that I was waiving my union recall right, which I agreed to do, I signed the document. Lastly, there were findings of fact made in the Cassino case stating that under Federal Rule of Evidence 408 the agreement was being admitted "as probative of the issue of discrimination," in other words to prove discrimination. In my case, there were no findings made by the district court judge related to the *November 1, 1985 document*, except for the fact that the district court judge stated he was letting the document in because it was probative on the issue of discrimination.

I have already explained many times in this chapter that an appellate court cannot *substitute its interpretation of the evidence for that of the trial court simply because the reviewing court might rule differently*. Moreover, the district court judge did not make any findings to explain how or why he found the *November 1, 1985 document* discriminatory, except that he did. These two appellate judges should have followed the ruling in the Cassino case, or remanded the case back to the district court judge for findings of fact as to why the district court judge believed the *November 1, 1985 document* was discriminatory. Again, these two appellate court judges knowingly acted outside their legal jurisdiction.

6) **The two appellate court judges in my case perpetrated fabrications to set aside the district court judge's findings of fact related to intentional racial employment discrimination.**

According to the case law that the two Ninth Circuit judges cited in my case, the parties at trial must litigate a contract issue, or the district court judge must grant a summary judgment motion with findings of fact based on the analysis of contract interpretation before a de novo review could be applied. These two appellate court judges stated in their ruling that the district court judge did not let either WCG or me submit any evidence on this document during the trial, which means that WCG and I did not litigate this issue at trial[40]. Therefore, for these two appellate judges to state that the "trial court record as a whole sufficiently establishes the voluntariness of the agreement" *is totally false and absurd.* It is irrational for these two appellate court judges to make a ruling like this when they also stated that the district court judge did not permit any evidence on this issue during the trial. Additionally, they lack the jurisdiction to review the *November 1, 1985 document* under the de novo standard because the district court judge did not state that he used an analysis of the contractual language and an application of the principles of contract interpretation, or made findings of fact stating the above. Nonetheless, these two appellate court judges go on to say that they would not remand my case back to Judge Tanner for findings of fact related to the *November 1, 1985 document.* I believe if they did, these two appellate judges

---

[40]   As stated earlier in chapter 12, Judge Tanner stated at the beginning of the trial that he did not want to hear anything that he already denied at the summary judgment level.

could not have done what Mr. Whitters asked the panel to do, which was to have them rule on the *November 1, 1985 document*, even though it was not litigated between the parties at trial and the Ninth Circuit panel had no legal jurisdiction over this issue.

Let us look at the other *untruth* that was perpetrated by these two judges in my case. On page 462 of these two appellate court judges' ruling they state, "**The district court's findings** pertaining to whether Stroman's waiver is valid are *reviewed under the clearly erroneous standard*" [emphasis added]. Then they stated, "See *Ahern*, 846 F.2d at 48." I have already shown that the only findings made by the district court in my case pertain to intentional racial employment discrimination and constructive discharge. Besides, it would be incongruous for an experienced district court judge like Judge Tanner to make findings of fact on an issue that was not litigated by the parties at trial, nor was a part of the trial court's transcripts. However, these two appellate court judges are saying that they can review the *November 1, 1985 document* under both the de novo review and now under the clearly erroneous review. There was not a case law cited by these two appellate court judges in which an appellate court panel reviewed an agreement under both the de novo standard and the clearly erroneous standard.

Nonetheless, let us look at the *Ahern* decision where the Ninth Circuit ruled, "The district court's **finding** that Schlegel assented to the settlement and intended to be bound by it must be affirmed unless it is clearly erroneous." Again, this ruling does not apply to my case because there were no district court findings of fact on a settlement agreement. This ruling could have been applied if Judge Tanner made findings of fact stating he was using extrinsic evidence to show discrimination related to the *November 1, 1985 document*. Since he only made findings of intentional racial employment discrimination and constructive discharge and **those findings are not clearly erroneous, then they must be affirmed.**

7) *The two appellate court judges in my case acted outside their judicial jurisdiction making them trespassers of the law.*

It is obvious that these two judges had to deceive the public into believing that findings related to a waiver of my federal rights were part of the intentional racial discrimination decision/findings by Judge Tanner. Since these two judges stated that there were findings on a waiver of my federal rights, it would only be just for these judges to produce Judge Tanner's findings on a waiver to prove that they did not act outside their judicial jurisdiction.[41] Without these findings of fact, it shows that these two judges did fabricate something that was untrue to set aside Judge Tanner's findings of intentional racial employment discrimination, and they intentionally caused harm to me, and my family. Furthermore, it shows that they acted outside of their judicial jurisdiction, making them "trespassers of the law."

In other words, in *Yates v. Village of Hoffman Estates*, 209 F.Supp 757 (1962), the court held that, "Not every action by any judge is in exercise of his judicial function. It is not a judicial function for a judge to commit an intentional tort even though the tort occurs in the courthouse."[42] In essence, when a judge does not follow the

---

[41] Remember these two judges used these imaginary findings to set aside Judge Tanner's Findings of fact against WCG, which was not according to Federal Civil Procedure Rule 52(a).

[42] According to Barron's Law Dictionary a "tort [is a] wrong; a private or civil wrong or injury resulting from a breach of a legal duty . . ."

law, the judge loses subject matter jurisdiction and the Judge's
Orders are void, of no legal force or effect . . . [and which] means
[the] Judge's ruling is void.[43] These two appellate court judges did
not act as judges, but as private individuals with their own personal
biases and prejudices when they *perpetrated* their fabrications to
set aside my district court findings of fact pertaining to intentional
racial employment discrimination. These two appellate judges'
action caused me harm, making it an intentional tort so their ruling
must be voided. All of the above should apply to the action by
these two federal appellate judges for perpetrating untruths to set
aside a ruling of a federal district court judge. In addition to their
action, they deprived me of my Constitutional right to due process
to litigate the issue of whether I waived my Title VII Rights under
the 1964 Civil Rights Act to sue my then employer.

8) *I believe the ruling by these two appellate court judges to set
   aside my district court judge's findings of intentional racial
   employment discrimination was racially motivated.*

---

[43]   Also, in *Scheuer v. Rhodes*, 416 U.S. 232, 249, 94 S.Ct. 1683, 40
       L.Ed.2d 90 (1974), the U.S. Supreme Court held, "There is no such
       avenue of escape from the paramount authority of the Federal
       Constitution. When there is a substantial showing that the exertion of
       State power (in my case judicial power) has overridden private rights
       secured by that Constitution, the subject is necessarily one for judicial
       inquiry in an appropriate proceeding." Additionally, in *U.S. v. Will*, 499
       U.S. 187, 222, 111 S.Ct. 1196 (1980), the Supreme Court held in that
       discrimination case, "It seems that if the Court of Appeals had properly
       analyzed that evidence, it would have concluded that summary
       judgment against petitioners was not appropriate because**1216 [sic]
       there was a dispute over a material issue of fact." In my case, the
       Court of Appeals did not properly analyze all of the evidence filed with
       the district court during the employer's summary judgment motions.

I believe these two appellate court judges' ruling was based on race. My beliefs are based on the following reasons:

(1) It was two white appellate judges who fabricated the ruling that Judge Tanner made **findings of fact** pertaining to the *November 1, 1985 document.*

(2) The fact that Judge Tanner, at that time, was the only black district court judge in the Western District of Washington and he ruled against a major white corporation on my allegations of intentional racial employment discrimination.

(3) These two appellate judges used the above untruths to set aside Judge Tanner's **findings of fact** related to my allegations of intentional racial employment discrimination against WCG, and these two appellate judges' action were not according to Federal Civil Procedure Rule and established federal case law.

(4) WCG's attorney did not want Judge Tanner to rule on the *November 1, 1985 document,* if the Ninth Circuit remanded my case back to him, based on his life experience as a black man. I say this, because WCG's attorney made the argument to this Ninth Circuit panel that, because Judge Tanner was a member of the black race, and perhaps had experienced discrimination, it meant that WCG was denied a fair trial (see exhibit #12). This last part shows the racism of WCG's attorneys, because I believe that they believe that only a white judge could make a proper ruling relating to the *November 1, 1985 document.* I furthermore believe, based on the ruling by these two judges within the Ninth Circuit that this perpetuates the belief that racism existed in the Ninth Circuit at that time, and still may exist.

(5) Since these two appellate court judges published this untrue ruling in my case, they are in effect telling every citizen, who is covered by race under Title VII law, "If you win at the district court level you stand a chance of running into discrimination at the appellate court level. As was shown in my case this could lead to a blatant miscarriage of justice," at least within the Ninth Circuit Court of Appeals.

Furthermore, this ruling basically means that I do not have the same rights as a criminal defendant in a correctional facility when it comes to the drafting and presentation of a waiver of federal rights. With a criminal defendant, a waiver of federal rights agreement would be drafted by an attorney, and the agreement would specifically state that the criminal defendant is waiving his/her federal right to a lawsuit or trial surrounding his/her allegations of violations of the individual's civil rights. Before the criminal defendant signed the agreement, it would also be explained to him/her, by an attorney, regardless of the fact that the criminal defendant had business related college classes, or whether or not he/she was in the military. After an attorney explained the waiver agreement, the criminal defendant would know exactly which federal rights he/she was waiving, and if he/she signed the waiver agreement, the signature would be knowingly, intentionally, and voluntarily executed.

The bottom line is, during the time that my case was assigned to Judge Tanner, he was an experienced trial court judge with many years on the bench (he has since passed). I am sure my case was not the first case that came before Judge Tanner that involved an allegation of a waiver of federal rights or Title VII claims. In essence, based on the fact that WCG is a major white corporation, Judge

Tanner is black, and these two appellate judges are white, the ruling by these two appellate court judges, to me, looks like race might have played a major part in these two Ninth Circuit Court of Appeals judges' ruling in my case. Especially when WCG's attorney argued that Judge Tanner should be replaced because he was black and might have experience racial discrimination, which would cause WCG to not receive a fair trial. What other reason would explain why these two federal appellate court judges would make a ruling like this in my case, knowing that they were acting outside their judicial jurisdiction? Additionally, their ruling perpetuated the belief that many blacks have toward white judges, which is, "when a white judge(s) does not want a black citizen to have something that he/she has earned, and/or to which he/she is constitutionally entitled, a white judge(s) has the power to break the law, or deny any rights that the black citizen might have under the law."

EXHIBIT #13

884 F.2d 458

50 Fair Empl.Prac.Cas. 1204,
51 Empl. Prac. Dec. P 39,293
Grady M. STROMAN, Plaintiff-Appellee,
v.
WEST COAST GROCERY COMPANY, Defendant-Appellant.

No. 88-3815.

**United States Court of Appeals,
Ninth Circuit.**

*Argued and Submitted Jan. 12, 1989.
Decided Aug. 31, 1989.*

Timothy J. Whitters, Seattle, Wash., for defendant–appellant.

J. Michael Gallagher, Seattle, Wash., for plaintiff–appellee.

Appeal from the United States District Court for the Western District of Washington.

Before WRIGHT, TANG and WIGGINS, Circuit Judges.

WIGGINS, Circuit Judge:

West Coast Grocery Company (West Coast) appeals from a judgment entered against it after a bench trial in this action under 42 U.S.C. Sec. 2000e (1982) brought by appellee Grady Michael Stroman. The district court held that Stroman was denied training for a supervisory position because he was black. The court also held that Stroman was constructively discharged as a result of the actions of several of Stroman's supervisors. The court awarded Stroman $291,445.88 in back and front pay. We reverse the district court's judgment because Stroman's suit was barred by the terms of the release agreement entered into by Stroman and West Coast.

* Stroman began working with West Coast as a part time order selector on January 15, 1981. Stroman's job as an order selector consisted of identifying pallets of groceries in West Coast's warehouse and transporting the pallets to different shipping locations throughout the warehouse. He was switched to full time on September 28, 1981.

Beginning in early 1982 Stroman made repeated requests to be trained for a position as a grocery warehouse supervisor in the scheduling office. An employee generally had to be recommended by his supervisors for training in the scheduling office. Stroman's supervisors declined to recommend him for training.

Stroman applied and was interviewed for a supervisor position in the scheduling office in April 1985. He was not selected. As a result of his failure to obtain the position, Stroman filed a discrimination charge with the Washington State Human Rights Commission (WSHRC) and the Equal Employment Opportunity Commission (EEOC) alleging that he was denied the position because of his race.

On June 12, 1985, Stroman filed a second discrimination charge alleging retaliation because of the previous charge. In July 1985 Stroman again applied for a supervisor position, but was not selected.

Stroman sought and obtained a voluntary medical leave of absence on August 5, 1985. In late October 1985, Stroman approached his supervisor Willy Mosley regarding the possibility of being put on economic layoff so that he could receive unemployment benefits. Although the economic layoff was meant only for part time employees, West Coast agreed to place Stroman on economic layoff status. In exchange West Coast required Stroman to enter into the following agreement:

West Coast Grocery and Grady Michael Stroman agree to the following:

1. Mike will leave the Company on an economic lay-off.

2. West Coast will not contest the unemployment benefits.

3. The employee's record will be cleared and information given out limited to date of hire, rate of pay, and journeyman status.

4. The employee will have no recall rights.

5. The employee will be entitled to any accrued vacation and his share of Profit Sharing payable as defined by Federal law, and the terms of the Profit Sharing Trust.

6. These terms represent a full and final settlement of any and all claims arising out of Mike's employment with West Coast Grocery.

The agreement, dated November 1, 1985, was signed by Stroman, Mosley, and David Hamlin, the Operations Manager for West Coast.

On December 2, 1985, Stroman filed a third discrimination charge alleging that West Coast failed to promote Stroman to the July 1985 supervisor position because of his race. Stroman filed this suit on July 31, 1986, alleging that he was denied training and promotion because of his race. He also stated a claim of retaliation and constructive discharge. During trial, the district court held that the November 1, 1985, agreement was a "termination of work" agreement and not a release of claims against West Coast. The court apparently based its conclusion on the fact that Stroman was still employed when he signed the agreement and no lawyers had yet become involved, and also because the statement contained in paragraph six that the agreement represented a "full and final settlement of any and all claims" did not explicitly mention Title VII. Concluding that it was a termination of work agreement, the court held that the agreement was admissible only to show discriminatory intent. See, Cassino v. Reichhold Chemicals, Inc., 817 F.2d 1338, 1342 (9th Cir.1987), cert. denied, --- U.S. ----, 108 S.Ct. 785, 98 L.Ed.2d 870 (1988).

The district court further held that West Coast's decision not to train Stroman was racially motivated, and that Stroman was constructively discharged because of the actions and conduct of West Coast. The court awarded Stroman $101,372.48 in back pay. The court also awarded Stroman $190,073.40 in front pay "due to corporate hostility" toward Stroman. This timely appeal followed. We have jurisdiction over this action under 28 U.S.C. Sec. 1291 (1982).

II

"A general release of Title VII claims does not ordinarily violate public policy. To the contrary, public policy favors voluntary settlement of employment discrimination claims brought under Title VII."[1] Rogers v. General Elec. Co., 781 F.2d 452, 454 (5th Cir.1986) (citations omitted); cf. Ahern v. Central Pac. Freight Lines, 846 F.2d 47, 48 (9th Cir.1988) (noting "overriding public interest in settling and quieting litigation" in action for securities and RICO violations). We nevertheless must closely scrutinize a waiver of rights under Title VII because of their remedial nature. See Freeman v. Motor Convoy, Inc., 700 F.2d 1339, 1352 (11th Cir.1983).

The interpretation and validity of a release of claims under Title VII is governed by federal law. See Salmeron v. United States, 724 F.2d 1357, 1361 (9th Cir.1983); see also Fulgence v. J. Ray McDermott & Co., 662 F.2d 1207, 1209 (5th Cir.1981) ("Creation of a federal rule rather than absorption of a state rule is appropriate where ... the rights of the litigants and the operative legal policies derive from a federal source."); cf. Jones v. Taber, 648 F.2d 1201, 1203 (9th Cir.1981) (federal law governs waiver of section 1983 claim). We first consider whether the agreement is properly interpreted as a termination of work agreement as the district court held, or whether as West Coast argues the agreement constitutes a valid waiver by Stroman of all legal claims against West Coast.

The district court's conclusion that the November 1, 1985, agreement did not constitute a release of all claims against West Coast was based primarily on an analysis of the contract provisions. We therefore review the district court's determination de novo. See Miller v. Safeco Title Ins. Co., 758 F.2d 364, 367-68 (9th Cir.1985); see also Marchese v. Shearson Hayden Stone, Inc., 734 F.2d 414, 417 (9th Cir.1984). We conclude that the agreement constitutes a clear and unambiguous waiver by Stroman of all legal claims against West Coast. Under the terms of the agreement, West Coast agreed to allow Stroman to leave the company on economic layoff so that he could collect unemployment benefits, clear Stroman's record, and limit the information given to prospective employers to the date of hire, rate of pay, and journeyman status. In exchange, Stroman agreed that the agreement would represent "a full and final settlement of any and all claims" arising out of his employment with West Coast. This language unambiguously indicates that Stroman intended to waive all claims against West Coast, including those then pending before the WSHRC and the EEOC.

The district court cited three reasons in support of its conclusion that the agreement was not a release of claims against West Coast. First, it relied on the absence of any mention of Title VII in paragraph six of the agreement. Contrary to the district court's conclusion, an agreement need not specifically recite the particular claims waived in order to be effective. The fact that Stroman's prior claims involved employment discrimination shows an intent to release Title VII claims under the agreement. The district court also based its interpretation of the agreement as a termination of work agreement on the fact that Stroman was still employed by West Coast when he signed the agreement. We fail to see the relevance of Stroman's work status in light of the unambiguous language of the contract. We do not believe that whether Stroman was technically still employed when he signed the agreement has any bearing on the agreement's interpretation. We reach the same conclusion with respect to the district court's observation that no lawyers were consulted in the drafting of the agreement. In any event, the district court's reasoning--that the absence of lawyers indicates that the agreement was not intended to relate to Stroman's legal claims--is undercut by Mosley's testimony at trial that he was aware of the substantive aspect of Title VII, although he did not know it by that name.

Our holding in Cassino v. Reichhold Chemicals, Inc., 817 F.2d 1338 (9th Cir.1987), cert. denied, --- U.S. ----, 108 S.Ct. 785, 98 L.Ed.2d 870 (1988), has little relevance to this case. In Cassino we concluded that a "settlement agreement and General Release" was properly admitted by the district court under Fed.R.Evid. 408 as probative of the issue of discrimination. Id. at 1342. For whatever reason, whether the plaintiff's suit was barred by the release was not at issue.[2] Here, the court erred in holding that the agreement was probative only of discrimination. The validly executed document should have been interpreted as a release barring the suit. Cassino is irrelevant to this case based on our holding that the agreement constitutes a release of Stroman's legal claims.

Our conclusion that the November 1, 1985, agreement constitutes a release of all Stroman's legal claims does not end the inquiry. We must also determine whether Stroman's release of his discrimination claims was a "voluntary, deliberate and informed" waiver. Salmeron, 724 F.2d at 1361; Taber, 648 F.2d at 1203; see also Alexander v. Gardner-Denver Co., 415 U.S. 36, 52 n. 15, 94 S.Ct. 1011, 1021 n. 15, 39 L.Ed.2d 147 (1974). The district court's findings pertaining to whether Stroman's waiver is valid are reviewed under the clearly erroneous standard. See Ahern, 846 F.2d at 48; (citing Worthy, 756 F.2d at 1372).

The determination of whether a waiver of Title VII was "voluntary, deliberate, and informed" is "predicated upon an evaluation of several indicia arising from the circumstances and conditions under which the release was executed." Coventry v. United States Steel Corp., 856 F.2d 514, 522 (3d Cir.1988); see Salmeron, 724 F.2d at 1362 (whether a release was voluntary must be determined from all the circumstances); Taber, 648 F.2d at 1203 (whether release was voluntary depends on both objective and subjective factors). Of primary importance in this calculation is the clarity and lack of ambiguity of the agreement, see Coventry, 856 F.2d at 522; Rogers, 781 F.2d at 455-56, the plaintiff's education and business experience, see Coventry, 856 F.2d at 523 (quoting EEOC v. American Express Publishing Corp., 681 F.Supp. 216, 219 (S.D.N.Y.1988)), "the presence of a noncoercive atmosphere for the execution of the release," Taber, 648 F.2d at 1204; see also Salmeron, 724 F.2d at 1362; Coventry, 856 F.2d at 523, and whether the employee had the benefit of legal counsel, see Salmeron, 724 F.2d at 1362; Taber, 648 F.2d at 1205; Coventry, 856 F.2d at 523.

Based on his ruling that the agreement was a termination of work agreement, the district court precluded West Coast's counsel from examining either Stroman or Mosley regarding the conditions under which the agreement was signed. The court did, however, permit West Coast's counsel to make an offer of proof incorporating Mosley's affidavit. We conclude that the record as a whole sufficiently establishes the voluntariness of the agreement and no purpose would be served by remanding the case to the district court to reconsider this issue.

We are satisfied that Stroman's release of "all claims" against West Coast under the November 1, 1985, agreement was a deliberate, voluntary, and knowing waiver of his Title VII and related claims. As we have previously indicated, the sixth paragraph of the agreement unambiguously indicates that Stroman intended to waive all legal claims against West Coast. We note that Stroman's work experience and college education were particularly relevant to our determination of a knowing and voluntary waiver. Although Stroman was not a sophisticated businessman, his training in the Army and his business management-related community college degree convince us that Stroman possessed the education and skills necessary to understand that when he signed the agreement he waived all legal claims against West Coast.[3] He was sufficiently intelligent to understand that "all claims" meant all legal claims, including claims brought under Title VII.

Additionally, there is no evidence whatsoever that Stroman was coerced into signing the agreement. To the contrary, it was Stroman who approached Mosley asking to be placed on economic layoff. When the agreement initially was presented to Stroman, he was not coerced into signing it. In fact, Stroman did not sign it until several days later. Although he did not have an attorney read the agreement before signing it, there is no evidence indicating that Stroman was discouraged or precluded from doing so. In fact, Mosley, who was not permitted by the district judge to testify on this issue, indicated in his affidavit that he asked Stroman whether he wished to have an attorney read the agreement before signing and that Stroman responded that he did not. We therefore conclude that the contractual agreement released Stroman's Title VII discrimination claims, and that the release was a deliberate and informed waiver.

III

For the foregoing reasons, we reverse the district court's judgment in favor of Stroman and order that judgment be entered in favor of West Coast and the action dismissed.[4]

REVERSED

TANG, Circuit Judge, dissenting in part:

I agree that the economic layoff agreement was sufficient to waive Stroman's Title VII claims. I dissent, however, from the majority's factual determination that Stroman waived his Title VII rights knowingly and voluntarily.

When an appellate court determines that a lower court made findings based upon an erroneous view of the law, the appellate court may not make contrary findings but must remand for new findings to be made in the light of the correct rule of law. Pullman-Standard v. Swint, 456 U.S. 273, 102 S.Ct. 1781, 72 L.Ed.2d 66 (1982). This is not a game where an incorrect understanding of the law by the fact finder results in automatic granting of relief. Such a rule would require inefficient use of limited resources because the district court would have to make factual determinations in every case regardless of whether they are needed.

The only exception to that rule is if "the record permits only one resolution of the factual issue". Id. citing Kelley v. Southern Pacific Co., 419 U.S. 318, 331-332, 95 S.Ct. 472, 479-80, 42 L.Ed.2d 498 (1974). The majority presumes that Stroman waived his Title VII rights knowingly and voluntarily but I do not believe that the record permits only one conclusion as to this matter.

I would therefore remand for a determination as to whether the waiver of Title VII rights was made knowingly and voluntarily. It is the fact-finder, not us, who should determine these issues in the first instance.

1

Whether "policies underlying [a federal] statute ... render [a] waiver unenforceable is a question of federal law." Newton v. Rumery, 480 U.S. 386, 392, 107 S.Ct. 1187, 1192, 94

L.Ed.2d 405 (1987). "[A] promise is unenforceable if the interest in its enforcement is outweighed in the circumstances by a public policy harmed by enforcement of the agreement." Id. (footnote omitted)

We perceive no public policy that would be harmed by enforcement of the November 1, 1985, agreement.

2

The document was never signed. Cassino, 817 F.2d at 1341-42

3

Significantly, Stroman relied on this background in applying for a supervisory position at West Coast

4

Because we hold that the November 1, 1985, agreement bars this suit, we need not address West Coast's other arguments

Chapter Sixteen

The Dissent by Judge Tang

Judge Tang did not agree with the two other judges and he requested that his dissenting ruling be published. Thus, it is available for anyone to read.[44] If Judge Tang would have agreed with the two other judges, then it would have been an unpublished ruling, and it could only be used in limited circumstances, such as demonstrating the existence of a conflict among opinions, dispositions, or orders.[45]

Judge Tang said in his dissent, which is part of the ruling cited in *Stroman v. West Coast Grocery,* "I dissent . . . from the majority's factual determination that Stroman waived his Title VII Rights knowingly and voluntarily."

Then he said in his dissent,

> The majority presumes that Stroman waived his Title VII Rights knowingly and voluntarily but I do not believe that the record permits only one conclusion as to this matter.[46]

Judge Tang's dissent also says,

> When an appellate court determines that a lower court made findings based upon an erroneous view of the law, the appellate court may not make contrary findings but

---

[44]   See Ninth Circuit Rule 36-2.

[45]   See Ninth Circuit Rule 36-3 c (iii).

[46]   Over the years I have always been confused which record Judge Tang is referring to, the docket sheet (which is the court record) or the actual trial court record (which is the trial court transcripts).

must remand for new findings to be made in the correct rule of law. Pullman-Standard v. Swint, 456 U.S. 273, 102 S.Ct. 1781, 72 L.Ed. 2d 66 (1982).

Lastly, he says,

> I would therefore remand for a determination as to whether the waiver of Title VII Rights were made knowingly and voluntarily. It is the fact-finder, "*not us*," who should determine these issues in the first instance.

Even though the evidence clearly shows that there were no findings by Judge Tanner pertaining to a waiver, Judge Tang's dissent also shows that these two federal circuit judges intentionally acted unjustly.

It is true that Judge Tanner did rule, without findings, that the *November 1, 1985 document* was a termination of work agreement, and held that the document was admissible only to show discriminatory intent. This fact can be easily proven by the dialogue between Judge Tanner and WCG's attorney, Mr. Whitters, pertaining to Federal Rule of Evidence 408 that was recorded on the trial court transcripts. Judge Tanner stated,

> In *Cassino v. Reichhold Chemicals, Inc.*, at 817 F.2d 1338, 1342, the Ninth Circuit ruled that, because Cassino had not asserted any claim at the time Reichhold asked for the release and, therefore, Rule 408 did not bar its admission.

Judge Tanner then stated, because I had not filed a complaint of racial employment discrimination in federal court I had not asserted any claims yet.

Additionally, filing with the EEOC is not the same as filing in federal court, because I had to file a charge of employment discrimination with the EEOC in order to obtain a right to sue letter before filing a complaint in federal court according to Congress. Furthermore, it is true that Judge Tanner's ruling was based upon the Ninth Circuit ruling in Cassino's case pertaining to the "Termination Agreement." The Ninth Circuit stated in the Cassino case,

> Such termination agreements are generally made a part of the record in the case and are considered relevant to the circumstances surrounding the alleged discriminatory discharge itself. The termination agreements, therefore, are probative on the issue of discrimination.

The dissenting judge established that if Judge Tanner made a ruling on the *November 1, 1985 document*, with findings, based upon an erroneous view of the law, these two circuit judges had to have known that they must remand the case back to Judge Tanner, in light of the correct rule of law.

It also seems peculiar that there was no mention by any of the three federal circuit court judges about WCG's summary judgment motion and reconciliation motion, pertaining to the *November 1, 1985 document*, in which Judge Tanner denied both motions without any written findings.

To me, it seems obvious why Judge Wright and Judge Wiggins would not mention the fact that there was both a summary judgment

motion and a reconsideration motion by WCG pertaining to the
November 1, 1985 document. It would show that Judge Tanner saw
memorandums of law from both parties' attorneys, saw affidavits
from Mosley, my witnesses, and me.[47] Also, Judge Tanner saw
evidence like the collective bargaining agreement which states
in part,

> . . . WCG agrees not to enter into any agreement or
> contract with the union members, which in any way
> conflicts with the terms and provisions of this Agreement.
> Any such agreement shall be null and void.

Upon reviewing the evidence, Judge Tanner denied WCG's
summary judgment motion and reconsideration motion pertaining
to the *November 1, 1985 document*. All of the above affidavits are
part of the trial court's docket sheet.

Since Judge Tanner had already seen enough evidence from
both sides, he was convinced that the *November 1, 1985 document*
was not signed knowingly and voluntarily by me, and maybe saw
it as discriminatory since no other order selector needed to waive
any rights to accept the lay-off offer.

I do not know why Judge Tang did not say in his opinion that
Judge Tanner denied both the summary judgment motion and a
reconsideration motion by WCG on the issue of a waiver. Moreover,
I do not know why Judge Tang did not just go ahead and state the
"truth" that there were no written findings pertaining to a waiver of
federal rights by Judge Tanner for the two other appellate court
judges to review. The only reason I can think of as to why Judge

---

[47]   A memorandum is an argument by an attorney in support of their
position.

Tang did not state this, would be because he would be saying that these two federal appellate judges knew they did not have jurisdiction in determining the issue of a waiver. This makes them *trespassers of the law* and *shows that they were perpetrating untruths.*

Judge Tang was correct when he said my case should be remanded back to Judge Tanner to make findings on the *November 1, 1985 document* "in the first instance," according to Federal Civil Procedure Rule 52, case law by the U.S. Supreme Court, as well as all the Ninth Circuit case laws and other Federal Courts of Appeals.

For the sake of argument, even if Judge Tanner did make findings saying that the *November 1, 1985 document* was probative only to show discrimination, according to the U.S. Supreme Court rulings in *Pullman-Standard v. Swint* and *Inwood Laboratories, Inc. et al., v. Ives Laboratories, Inc.,*[48]

> In reviewing the factual findings of the District Court, the Court of Appeals was bound by the clearly erroneous standard of Rule 52(a), Federal Rules of Civil Procedure. That Rule recognizes and rests upon the unique opportunity afforded the trial court judge to evaluate the credibility of witnesses and to weigh the evidence.

Therefore, when these two appellate court judges determined that Judge Tanner made findings pertaining to the *November 1, 1985*

---

[48]   Pullman-Standard v. Swint, 456 U.S. 273, 102 S.Ct.1781, 72 L.Ed.2d 66(1982), and Inwood Laboratories, Inc. et al., v. Lves Laboratories, Inc. Darby Drug Co., Inc, et al v. Lves Laboratories, Inc. 456 U.S. 844, 102 S.Ct. 2182, 72 L.Ed.2d 606 (1982).

document that was based upon an erroneous view of the law, these two appellate court judges cannot make contrary findings but must remand for new findings to be made in the light of the correct rule of law. Furthermore, Rule 52 recognizes and rests *upon the unique opportunity afforded the trial court judge* to evaluate the credibility of witnesses and to weigh the evidence. There is nothing in Rule 52 stating that appellate court judges can evaluate the credibility of witnesses or weigh evidence.

I believe that Judge Wiggins and Wright must have felt confident that they would face no consequences for acting outside their judicial jurisdiction, especially when Judge Tang did not contradict their assertion that Judge Tanner had made findings of fact about whether or not I waived my federal rights. They must have known that they would face no consequences for *perpetrating* intentional lies, even though this would lead to a miscarriage of justice in my case. Also, they must have felt confident that no other judge within the Ninth Circuit, or U.S. Supreme Court would question their falsehood particularly once they published it, which perpetuated the belief that white judges will break the law with no consequences when it comes to a black person. This supports the widely held opinion that white judges will go as far as to break the law when dealing with black people, knowing that they will face no consequences.

The actions by Senior Circuit Judge Wright and Circuit Judge Wiggins pertaining to my case reminded me of something I read by Fredrick Douglass, the former slave and great African American writer, when he described the American criminal justice system as follows,

> Justice is often painted with bandaged eyes. She is
> described in forensic eloquence, as utterly blind to wealth
> or poverty, high or low, white or black, but a mask of iron,
> however thick, could never blind American justice, when
> a black man happens to be on trial.[49]

These two federal circuit judges showed me that it is the same in some civil cases as in criminal cases that justice is not blind when it comes to a black person.

For the integrity of Title VII of the 1964 Civil Rights Act, it should be important that a federal court of appeals uphold Federal Civil Procedure Rule 52. This should be particularly of concern when it involves a federal district judge not making findings of fact when denying an employer's motion for summary judgment base on an allegation by the employer of a waiver of the employee's Title VII claims to sue the employer.

---

[49] "Frederick Douglass, the orator: containing an account of his life; his eminent public services; his brilliant career as orator; selections from his speeches and writing," by James Monroe Gregory (1893).

Chapter Seventeen

My Appeal to the entire 9ᵗʰ Circuit Court of Appeals

By the time my attorney filed his brief to the Ninth Circuit, in **September 1989**, which requested Circuit Judges Wright and Wiggins to reconsider their ruling; I was a lot more knowledgeable of the Ninth Circuit case law, relating to the jurisdiction of an appellate court panel.[50] My attorney asked the two appellate court judges to reconsider their ruling based on the fact that Judge Tanner made no findings of fact related to a waiver. Furthermore, the trial court record/transcripts are void of any oral testimony from the parties on this issue, although Judge Tanner denied both WCG's summary judgment and reconsideration motion on the issue of a waiver without findings of fact according to Federal Civil Procedure Rule 52.

The two judges would not change their ruling, so in **October 1989**, my attorney appealed to the entire Ninth Circuit Court of Appeals through a motion called an "En Banc" motion. An En Banc motion is requested by one of the litigants to have the full court consider the matter. The litigant who requests the motion only needs one judge out of all of the judges within that particular circuit to vote in his/her favor to have the En Banc motion granted.

Based on Judge Tang's dissenting opinion, my attorney asked the whole Ninth Circuit Court of Appeals to rule that it was not proper for these two appellate judges to rule on a summary judgment motion issue that was not part of the trial, or the trial court record/transcripts. In addition, all three appellate court judges knew the district federal judge made no findings on the issue of a waiver in his findings of fact and conclusion of law. We wanted the Ninth

---

[50] U.S. Supreme Court case law states that the district court makes findings of fact, and not the appellate court. Additionally, an appellate court panel can only review findings of fact made by the district court after a trial or summary judgment motion.

Circuit to rule that the two judges should have remanded the case back to Judge Tanner to make factual findings as to why there was no waiver of federal rights by me. In addition, we expected them to request that Judge Tanner explain why he ruled during the trial that he was only allowing the *November 1, 1985 document* into the trial court record/transcripts to show discrimination. The trial court record/transcripts and the two appellate court judges' ruling state that Judge Tanner relied on the Ninth Circuit Court ruling in the Cassino case pertaining to the discriminatory nature of some termination agreements.

We believed Judge Tang would provide the one vote we needed for an En Banc hearing based on his dissent, in which he stated,

> I would therefore remand the case back to Judge Tanner for a determination as to whether the waiver of Title VII rights was made knowingly, and voluntarily. It is the fact-finder, not us, who should determine these issues in the first instance.

He made the same statement during my motion for reconsideration to the appeal court panel. Nonetheless, in response to the En Banc motion, he stated that he did not believe the issues in my case were significant enough for the whole Ninth Circuit to hear. In other words, he did not believe the injustice committed by Judge Wright and Judge Wiggins was compelling, or that my constitutional right to due process was important. It is amazing to me that in the Ninth Circuit it is no major issue for judges not to tell the truth. Furthermore, no judge on the Ninth Circuit would vote to remand my case back to Judge Tanner to make findings of fact as to why he denied WCG's summary judgment motions on this waiver issue.

With all of the case law cited in the ruling by these two appellate court judges, *there is not one case that gives an appellate court panel the jurisdiction to dismiss a case on an issue that was not litigated at trial.* Lastly, I could not believe that none of the judges on the Ninth Circuit Court of Appeals, including Judge Tang, was willing to make the two circuit judges produce the findings of fact that they claimed they reviewed pertaining to a waiver of Title VII Rights by Judge Tanner.

It was therefore the responsibility of the entire Ninth Circuit to remand the case back to the district court judge, and by not doing so the whole Circuit has violated U.S. Supreme Court rulings. In addition, when the two appellate judges state at page 462 (2) of their ruling, "The district court's findings pertaining to whether Stroman's waiver is valid are reviewed under the clearly erroneous standard." (See *Ahern*, 846 F.2d at 48.) They knew according to the 1988 ruling by the Ninth Circuit in *Ahern's* case, which they cited in my case, that they were violating a ruling from their own circuit because there were no findings by Judge Tanner relating to a settlement (waiver) to be reviewed under the clearly erroneous standard.[51] Moreover, the Ninth Circuit did not rule in this case that an appellate court panel could make contrary findings to the district court findings on a settlement (waiver) agreement if the district court judge's findings were clearly erroneous.

In the Ahern case, the Ninth Circuit stated in their ruling,

---

[51] In this case, the district court held an extensive evidentiary hearing on a settlement issue. Based on that record the district court affirmed the settlement. In my case, after two extensive summary judgment motions on a settlement issue and based on that record the district denied WCG's motion on this issue, without findings of fact, and let the case proceed to trial.

The Ninth Circuit is firmly committed to the rule that the law favors and encourages compromise settlements. United States v. McInnes, 556 F.2d 436, 441 (9th Cir. 1977). There is an overriding public interest in settling and quieting litigation. Id. (citations omitted). It is well recognized that settlement agreements are judicially favored as a matter of sound public policy. Settlement agreements conserve judicial time and limit expensive litigation. *Speed Shore Corp. v. Denda*, 605 F.2d 469, 473 (9th Cir. 1979).

Based on the ruling in my case it seems the two appellate judges believed the Ninth Circuit was saying that it is an overriding public interest to settle and quiet litigation concerning racial employment discrimination. Since the Ninth Circuit would not hold an En Banc hearing on the lie (fraud), committed by the two judges within that circuit, then I believe the Ninth Circuit supports what these two judges did. Moreover, I believe with the published ruling in my case, the Ninth Circuit is saying that if a black plaintiff does not settle their Title VII complaints with their white employer, this Court might let its judges create a lie to reverse a district court judge's findings of fact of intentional racial employment discrimination by the white employer. This is especially true, if the trial court judge is black. I say this because I believe the chances of these two appellate judges fabricating the frauds to set aside the same ruling, that I was a victim of intentional racial employment discrimination, by one of the many white federal district judges within the Western District of Washington are very unlikely.[52] On the other hand, since

---

[52] My beliefs are mainly based on exhibit #12.

Judge Tanner was the only black judge within the Western District of Washington at that time, I believe the Ninth Circuit is saying that he does not have the authority or ability to rule against a white corporation when it comes to allegations of intentional racial employment discrimination. I believe this is a deliberate insult to Judge Tanner, as well as to his ability as a federal district judge, to rule on an intentional racial employment discrimination matter according to the law.

After the Ninth Circuit's refusal to remand the case back to Judge Tanner, my attorney, Mike Gallagher started saying that the only reason I won at the summary judgment level was that both Judge Tanner and I are black. I said to Gallagher,

> Are you telling me that a white federal judge would not see from the evidence that was presented to Judge Tanner that Mosley made the offer of the lay-off to all of the warehouse order selectors? That a white federal judge would not see that I never filed a withdrawal form with the EEOC, or the WSHRC stating that I was willing to waive my Title VII complaints against WCG? That a white judge would not see that this *November 1, 1985 document* is in conflict with the collective bargaining agreement WCG had with the Teamster Union? Or that a white federal judge would say, okay WCG, I believe your version pertaining to the *November 1, 1985 document* over the evidence that Mr. Stroman has presented and will grant your summary judgment motion because we are white?

Gallagher said that is what these two judges on the Ninth Circuit just ruled; since the whole Ninth Circuit Court of Appeals refused to hear my case, all of the other judges in that circuit are stating that they do not care what the evidence shows, they are not going to overturn the two white judges ruling. Gallagher also said from this ruling, the whole Ninth Circuit Court of Appeals has told me that regardless of whether I proved intentional racial discrimination and constructive discharge, they were not going to let me win, even if these two federal circuit judges were breaking federal civil procedure rules, or committing lies (frauds). Gallagher lastly said that he was "done with my case," and was "not going to file a writ of certiorari on my behalf to the U.S. Supreme Court"[53]. Again, I was shown that the handling of my case comes down to race and not the facts and merits involved in it, and *exemplifies* and *perpetuates* the racism still within the U.S. judicial system.

In chapter 18, I talked about the Ninth Circuit Court of Appeals unpublished ruling in *Parker v. Suzuki Motor Corporation*, which was decided after my case, to use as a comparison of race based justice.[54] I believe the injustice and racism that happened in my case becomes clear after one reads the ruling in Parker's case.

---

[53]   The U.S. Supreme Court can issue this writ to any court in the land to review a federal question if at least one justice votes to hear the case. After Gallagher quit my case, I talked to a law professor at the University of Puget Sound Law School surrounding the unjust ruling related to my case. He agreed with me about the injustice and filed a writ of certiorari on my behalf, and helped me file a writ of mandamus to the U.S. Supreme Court. Surprisingly, the U.S. Supreme Court denied both writs. It seems that there is a **code of silence** when a case is decided according to race and not according to the law.

[54]   Race based justice is a case that was decided by race and not by the law.

Lastly, to show how **scandalous** WCG's attorneys are—and knowing the Ninth Circuit saved WCG hundreds of thousands of dollars—Elizabeth Martin (acting on WCG's behalf), filed a motion in the Court of Appeals for the Ninth Circuit to have me reimburse her law firm in the **amount of $1,265.10** for it's costs for bond and the appeal.[55] She could not wait to kick me while I was down, so she filed this motion on September 13, 1989—two weeks after the Ninth Circuit made its ruling against me. However, neither the Ninth Circuit nor Judge Tanner ever issued an order stating that I had to reimburse this law firm. This was not good enough for this law firm, so a motion was filed in Pierce County Superior Court for the collection of the above amount. I cannot remember the exact date that I received the copy of the complaint and subpoena that was delivered by a court marshal to the house that my family was renting. I responded to the complaint by saying I never received any order from Judge Tanner saying that I owed this money. Besides, Judge Tanner, Elizabeth Martin, and I all know that lies (frauds) were committed by the Ninth Circuit to set aside Judge Tanner's findings of fact of intentional racial employment discrimination against her law firm's client WCG. Nevertheless, if this law firm can produce the alleged findings of fact pertaining to a waiver of my federal rights by Judge Tanner, supposedly reviewed by the Ninth Circuit, then I would theoretically owe this money. After I filed my response there was no more action on this issue.

---

[55]   From the law offices of Gordon, Thomas, Honeywell, Malancia, Peterson & Daheim.

Chapter Eighteen

Inference of Race Based Justice
(The 9th Circuit ruling in Parker v.
Suzuki Motor Corporation)

After the Supreme Court denied my petitions, I went to the law library to find out if the Ninth Circuit had made any ruling on a "Release and Settlement Agreement" since the Cassino ruling and my case. To my surprise, I found an unpublished ruling to support my allegation relating to inference of race-based justice within the Ninth Circuit Court of Appeals. The *Parker v. Suzuki Motor Corporation* case, numbers 90-55056, 90-55179, was argued and submitted to the Ninth Circuit Court of Appeals on **October 9, 1991** and was decided by the Ninth Circuit Court of Appeals on **December 27, 1991(see exhibit 14)**. This was an unpublished ruling by the Ninth Circuit Court of Appeals because there was no dissenting opinion within the three-judge panel in this case. This means all three judges agreed that the correct rule of law had not been applied concerning a knowing, intentional, and voluntary waiver of Title VII Rights by the district court in this case.

In this case, Parker, who was a vice-president of Suzuki Motor Corporation *signed a release of all claims* against Suzuki that was negotiated by his attorney and Suzuki, and was later drafted by his attorney. At first, the district court denied Suzuki Motor Corporation's summary judgment motion, but later at a hearing for Suzuki's motion on reconsideration of the order to deny summary judgment stated,

> Suzuki responded that under **Stroman**, a party must be held to have intended to release all claims, including ADEA claims, if the release is unambiguous.

Afterwards, the district court granted Suzuki's motion based on its reading of **Stroman,** and made findings according to Federal

Civil Procedure Rule 56 in favor of Suzuki Motor Corporation[56]. What I earlier thought might happen occurred in the Parker case whereby the district court judge granted summary judgment for the employer based only on the criteria set by these two appellate judges in my case[57].

Afterward, Parker appealed this ruling to the Ninth Circuit Court of Appeals. It took the Ninth Circuit Court of Appeals less than three months to reverse the district court ruling and rule that the *signed waiver* in this case must be remanded back to the district court for **findings of fact** on whether the waiver was knowingly and voluntarily *signed*.[58] The Ninth Circuit Court of Appeals ruling in *Parker's* case says in part,

> In the first summary judgment hearing, the district court concluded that an issue of fact existed regarding whether

[56] "We note that Stroman's work experience and college education were particularly relevant to our determination of a knowing and voluntary waiver . . . . He was sufficiently intelligent to understand that all claims meant all legal claims, including claims brought under Title VII."

[57] All that is needed is that a plaintiff did read an agreement and has enough intelligence to understand what they had read, not the several indicia arising from the circumstances and conditions under which the release was executed, as in the ruling in EEOC v. American Express Publishing Corp where six criteria were established.

[58] After one reads the Parker ruling by the Ninth Circuit panel, the panel does not mention anything related to a district court findings of fact that Stroman knowingly, voluntarily, and intentionally waived his federal rights to sue WCG. However, they remand the case back to the district court judge in Parker's case to do exactly that. Furthermore, after reading Parker's case, one can "presumptively" conclude that Parker had an ADEA charge with EEOC prior to filing his complaint in federal court.

Parker knowingly and voluntarily released his ADEA
rights, because the release did not contain an express
waiver of Parker's ADEA rights.

Later the court held,

It is not clear to us whether the district court interpreted
Stroman as holding that a general release of "all claims"
includes a waiver of an ADEA claim, without the necessity
to show that such waiver was deliberate, knowing, and
voluntary. [emphasis added]

Then the Ninth Circuit goes on to state, ". . . **Stroman** requires
that the record show that the employee deliberately intended to
waive his or her . . . rights" [emphasis added].[59] Parker's ruling
went on to say,

Because the record does not demonstrate whether, in
signing a release of "all claims" . . . Parker deliberately
intended to waive his ADEA claims, we must . . .

---

[59]   In my case, the rule of law was changed from 'findings of fact' by a
district court on whether I deliberately intended to waive my rights, to
somewhere on the record I deliberately intended to waive my rights.
This illustrates that judges within the Ninth Circuit Court of Appeals
will perpetuate a dishonest ruling by judges within that Circuit.

remand . . . regarding whether Parker deliberately, knowingly, and voluntarily intended to waive his ADEA claims.[60]

Even though this panel ruled that a district court judge needed to make findings on whether Parker voluntarily and willfully waived his ADEA claims, the panel ruling is an unpublished ruling. This means, as stated in the ruling,

> Ninth Circuit Rule 36-3 provides that dispositions other than opinions or orders designated for publication are not precedential and should not be cited except when relevant under the doctrines of law of the case, res judicata, or collateral estoppel.

This means another case could cite my case and the Parker's case in a petition, in order to demonstrate the existence of a conflict among the opinion in Parker's and my cases.[61] This is exactly what I am doing in my story—demonstrating the existence of a conflict due to the difference in the handling of the same rule of law between Parker's case and mine. My case also demonstrates a conflict between all of the other cases that have been mentioned

---

[60] In my case, the record demonstrates the district court judge would not let the parties introduce any oral testimony during the trial related to the November 1, 1985 document. This means that the issue of a waiver could not have been part of the trial court's record. However, the trial court's record does demonstrate the debates between the district court judge and WCG's lead attorney, on why the district judge believes the November 1, 1985 document was probative on the issue of discrimination.

[61] See Ninth Circuit Rule 36-3 c (iii).

in this story, in which the district court made findings of fact related to a waiver agreement of federal rights or Title VII claims. Furthermore, a conflict arises when a district court judge is not convinced that a valid waiver exists and makes no written findings on this issue.

The ruling in Parker shows that there are two different standards between me, a race discrimination plaintiff, and Parker, an age discrimination plaintiff, pertaining to a *signed agreement of "all claims."* Because the Ninth Circuit is comparing what the two appellate court judges stated was on my trial court record to Parker's summary judgment record; this is like comparing apples to oranges. I have already stated and shown that Judge Tanner denied WCG's summary judgment motion and reconsideration motion on the issue of a waiver of my Title VII Rights without findings. In addition, he did not allow WCG or me to argue during trial in order to establish whether the *November 1, 1985 document* was a knowing, intentional, and voluntary waiver of my Title VII Rights when I signed it. In addition, the district court judge in my case was also concerned that the *November 1, 1985 document* did not contain an express waiver of my Title VII Rights.

A true comparison between my case and Parker's case would be to review the evidence in the court record during the summary judgment motion and the reconsideration motion in both of our cases. Because Parker's case had not yet made it to the trial court level, when the Ninth Circuit made its ruling, any impartial federal judge with limited experience who looks at the court docket sheet in my case (along with the memorandums of law from both parties, the affidavits and evidence related to the summary judgment and reconsideration of motion) could see why Judge Tanner did not believe that *I knowingly, intentionally, and voluntarily waived my Title VII Rights.* In addition, from the same above affidavits on the court docket sheet, any impartial federal judge with limited experience would easily see that WCG's affidavits lacked credibility, based on the affidavits of my witnesses, and therefore determine that the document was discriminatory. Furthermore, if anyone reads the trial court transcripts they would see that Judge Tanner did not, and would not; let the issue of the *November 1, 1985 document* be litigated between the parties during the trial. Nonetheless, in my case these two judges went on to say, "No purpose would be served by remanding (my) case to the district court to reconsider this issue."

The Parker case shows that the dissenting judge in my case was correct when he said that it is the fact-finder (the trial court judge) and not the appellate court who makes the determination as to whether the waiver of Title VII Rights (race or ADEA) was made knowingly and voluntarily in the first instance.

The comparison between Parker's and my case shows that Parker received what I consider "white" race based justice and I received "black" race based justice by the Ninth Circuit Court of Appeals. Parker was given the opportunity to have a district court judge make findings on whether there was a knowing, deliberate, and intentional waiver of federal rights when he lost at the summary judgment level. However, in my racial discrimination case the district court judge denied the defendant's summary judgment motion and reconsideration motion as to whether there was a knowing, deliberate, and intentional waiver without findings. Additionally, in my case the Ninth Circuit ruled on the "waiver issue" without any findings by the district court judge.

In addition, in my case the Ninth Circuit ruled:

1) A clear and unambiguous waiver need not specifically recite Title VII in order to be effective;

2) That a company warehouse supervisor who did not recognize the name *Title VII* when questioned by the trial court judge was enough to show that the supervisor is knowledgeable of *Title VII Rights,*

3) That lawyers, or I, need not be involved in drafting a document for the intent of signing away *Title VII Rights,*

4) That because I filed discrimination charges with EEOC, I asserted federal claims, and

5) That a signed waiver cannot be probative on the issue of discrimination.

So in essence, for the Ninth Circuit to rule a race discrimination plaintiff waived his/her rights under Title VII:

1) A settlement agreement document need not be informative;

2) Lawyers, or the employee, need not be involved in drafting the settlement agreement;

3) Whether or not a waiver has been signed a district court judge needs not to look at evidence to determine if the waiver is probative on the issue of discrimination;

4) **Findings of fact** are needed from a district court judge when the district court denies the defendant's summary judgment motion on a waiver, even though Federal Civil Procedure Rule 52 states findings are unnecessary on a motion; and moreover

5) A Ninth Circuit panel can make findings on a waiver issue that was not litigated by the parties during a trial based on the de novo standard, and then look only at an affidavit submitted by the defendant (to which the trial court judge gave no credence).

The *Cassino* case, the *Parker* case, and my case all show that there is not consistency in the application of the law under Title VII of the 1964 Civil Rights Act by the Ninth Circuit Court of Appeals pertaining to employment discrimination cases.

Since all of the Ninth Circuit Judges refused to hear my case and the U.S. Supreme Court denied hearing both of my writs, their actions now make me think of the *Dred Scott* case [*Dred Scott v. Sandford*, 60 U.S. 393 (1857)]. This was a major landmark decision by the U.S. Supreme Court pertaining to the civil rights of Black Americans. The following is an excerpt of that ruling.

In 1857, Chief Justice Roger B. Tancy wrote for the majority of the U.S. Supreme Court, in the Dred Scott case. He said ". . . We think they [people of African Ancestry] are . . . not included, and were not intended to be included, under the word "citizens" in the Constitution, and can therefore claim none of the rights and privileges which that instrument provides for and secures to citizens of the United States . . ." Chief Justice Tancy went on to say, ". . . The framers of the Constitution believe that Blacks "had no rights which the white man was bound to . . ."

In fact, the *Dred Scott* decision was never overruled; it was superseded in 1865 by the passage of the Thirteenth Amendment that abolished slavery, and in 1868 by the passage of the Fourteenth Amendment that guaranteed full rights and citizenship regardless of race. In spite of these amendments, since the *Dred Scott* case many U.S. citizens still say that many of the U.S. Judicial rulings are race-based rulings. I have shown by actual documentation, because both Judge Tanner and myself are black, I received "black justice" (or at least injustice) by the Ninth Circuit Court of Appeals and the U.S. Supreme Court. The justice I received is similar to Chief Justice Tancy's ruling where he said in part, ". . . The framers of the Constitution believe that Blacks had no rights which the white man was bound to . . . ," these two white appellant judges demonstrated that Judge Tanner and I had no rights that they were bound to.

EXHIBIT #14

952 F.2d 407

NOTICE: Ninth Circuit Rule 36-3 provides that dispositions
other than opinions or orders designated for publication are not
precedential and should not be cited except when relevant under
the doctrines of law of the case, res judicata, or collateral
estoppel.

Albert PARKER, Plaintiff/Cross-Defendant and Appellant/Cross-
Appellee,

v.

U.S. SUZUKI MOTOR CORPORATION, et al.,
Defendant/Cross-Complainant and Appellee/Cross-Appellant,

Nos. 90-55056, 90-55179.

United States Court of Appeals, Ninth Circuit.

Argued and Submitted Oct. 9, 1991.
Decided Dec. 27, 1991.

Before JAMES R. BROWNING, ALARCON and T.G. NELSON, Circuit Judges.

MEMORANDUM*

Albert Parker alleged that American Suzuki Motor Corporation (Suzuki) fired him
because of his age in violation of the Age Discrimination in Employment Act
(ADEA), 29 U.S.C. §§ 621-634. Parker also alleged that he signed a release of all
claims against Suzuki under duress. Suzuki filed a counterclaim requesting a
judgment for breach of contract, specific performance, rescission, and fraud. Parker
appeals from the district court's grant of summary judgment in favor of Suzuki.
Suzuki appeals from the dismissal of its counterclaim.

We reverse the district court's grant of summary judgment in favor of Suzuki
because we conclude that the moving party failed to demonstrate that Parker
deliberately intended to waive his ADEA rights. We reverse the dismissal of
Suzuki's counterclaim because the court dismissed it without any proof that Suzuki
had failed to prosecute it or violated any court rule or order.

I. DISCUSSION

A. Failure to object to findings does not waive claim that genuine issue of
material fact exists

Suzuki argues that no genuine issue of material fact remains because Parker
failed to object to the district court's finding that the release was valid in its order
denying Suzuki's summary judgment motion. Suzuki cites no authority for this
proposition. A grant of summary judgment is reviewed de novo. See Schneider v.
TRW, Inc., No. 89-56160, slip op. 12301, 12307 (9th Cir. July 10, 1991, as amended,
August 27, 1991). Thus, we must determine independently whether a genuine issue

of material fact exists precluding summary judgment. Accordingly, the findings of the trial court have no bearing on our duty to examine the entire record to determine for ourselves whether there is a genuine issue of material fact in dispute.

B. A contract was formed

Parker alleges that Suzuki had not signed the release agreement prior to sending a letter on January 19, 1988, requesting a change in the original agreement. Parker argues that this letter was a counterproposal. Suzuki asserts that it accepted the release on December 23, 1987, by ordering the transfer of settlement funds to Parker's bank account.

Suzuki contends that this conduct was an acceptance of the release agreement drafted by Parker's counsel. It is not disputed that Suzuki had substantially fulfilled its contractual obligations on December 23, 1987. In California "[a]cceptance of an offer by conduct constitutes acceptance or assent in the view of the law." Logoluso v. Logoluso, 233 Cal.App.2d 523, 529 (1965); Coleman Engineering Company, Inc. v. North American Aviation, Inc., 65 Cal.2d 396, 411 (1966) (Traynor, C.J., dissenting). The record demonstrates that Suzuki accepted the release agreement by its conduct on December 23, 1987.

C. No genuine issues of material fact exist as to alleged threat

In a declaration submitted in opposition to Suzuki's motion for a summary judgment, Parker alleged that M. Tani, President of Suzuki, and Duffern Helsing, attorney for Suzuki, told Parker that he had to sign the agreement within three days or he would be fired with none of the "benefits" listed therein. Parker asserts that this statement constituted an improper threat to deprive him of his vested rights to a pension, vacation pay, and accrued salary.

Accepting the facts in the light most favorable to Parker, we conclude that Parker has failed to raise a genuine issue of material fact regarding his claim of duress. To survive a motion for summary judgment, Parker must "make a showing sufficient to establish the existence of an element essential to [his] case, and on which [he] will bear the burden of proof at trial." Celotex Corp. v. Catrett, 477 U.S. 317, 322 (1986). As the moving party, he will meet his burden of persuasion if he has offered sufficient evidence of a material fact such that "a reasonable jury could return a verdict for [him]." Anderson v. Liberty Lobby, Inc., 477 U.S. 242, 248 (1986). Where such evidence is merely colorable or is not significantly probative, however, summary judgment is properly granted. See id. at 249-50.

"Benefits" that are bargained for in negotiating a release agreement differ from vested rights to a pension, to vacation pay, or to accrued salary. The proposed release agreement provided for the use of a company car for six months and a lump sum severance payment. As a vice-president of Suzuki, Parker must be assumed to have been familiar with the distinction between vested rights and a bargained-for consideration to induce him to terminate his employment and to sign a release. The fact that Parker retained a lawyer who negotiated and drafted the release agreement further undermines Parker's claim of duress as of the time he signed the release agreement. See Stroman v. West Coast Grocery, 884 F.2d 458, 462 (9th Cir.1989), cert. denied, 111 S.Ct. 151 (1990) (whether employee had benefit of counsel is one factor determining voluntariness of waiver). In light of his extensive business experience and the fact that his attorney drafted the release agreement, Parker's allegation that he signed the release agreement because he felt threatened by the loss of his vested rights to a pension, to vacation pay, and to accrued salary is not sufficient evidence to persuade a reasonable jury by a preponderance of the evidence that Parker was acting under duress when he signed the release.

D. Unsupervised waivers of ADEA claims allowed

Parker contends that a waiver of an ADEA claim that was not supervised by the Equal Employment Opportunity Commission (EEOC) is invalid pursuant to the Fair Labor Standards Act, 29 U.S.C. §§ 201-219.

We conclude that a waiver of an ADEA claim is not invalid solely because it was unsupervised by the EEOC. In Gilmer v. Interstate/Johnson Lane Corp., 111 S.Ct. 1647 (1991), the Supreme Court noted that "nothing in the ADEA indicates that Congress intended that the EEOC be involved in all employment disputes. Such disputes can be settled, for example, without any EEOC involvement." Id. at 1653. The Court cited the following cases, each of which has held that a waiver of an ADEA claim is valid without EEOC supervision: Coventry v. United States Steel Corp., 856 F.2d 514, 522 (3rd Cir.1988); Moore v. McGraw Edison Co., 804 F.2d 1026, 1033 (8th Cir.1986); Runyan v. National Cash Register Corp., 787 F.2d 1039, 1045 (6th Cir.), cert. denied, 479 U.S. 850 (1986).

E. The district court erroneously construed Stroman's analysis

Parker contends that the district court was required under Stroman to inquire into Parker's intent to release his ADEA rights but failed to do so. Suzuki responds that under Stroman, a party must be held to have intended to release all claims, including ADEA claims, if the release is unambiguous.

In Stroman, we held that an employee had waived his Title VII claims by signing a general release that did not explicitly mention Title VII. We concluded in Stroman that the fact that the employee had filed several employment discrimination charges with the EEOC and other agencies before signing the release sufficiently showed an intent to release Title VII claims under the agreement. See 884 F.2d at 461. Although we concluded that an agreement "need not specifically recite the particular claims waived in order to be effective," we did not hold that a general release presumptively includes Title VII claims. Id. We noted in Stroman that a showing that the employee intended to waive Title VII claims is not enough. See id. at 462. We held that, to be valid, the record must show that the waiver of Title VII claims was "voluntary, deliberate and informed." Id. Citing Coventry v. United States Steel Corp., 856 F.2d 514 (3rd Cir.1988), inter alia, we listed in Stroman several criteria to be evaluated in determining whether the agreement was a deliberate, voluntary, and knowing waiver of the employee's Title VII claims. See 884 F.2d at 462. These factors include the clarity and lack of ambiguity of the agreement, the plaintiff's education and business experience, the presence of a noncoercive atmosphere, and whether the employee had the benefit of legal counsel. See id. We concluded in Stroman that the record showed that the employee's waiver had been deliberate, knowing, and voluntary.

The district court appears to have concluded that our decision in Stroman did not require Suzuki to make a showing in this summary judgment proceeding that Parker expressly intended to waive his specific ADEA claims. In the first summary judgment hearing, the district court concluded that an issue of fact existed regarding whether Parker knowingly and voluntarily released his ADEA rights, because the release did not contain an express waiver of Parker's ADEA rights.

At the hearing for Suzuki's motion on reconsideration of the order denying summary judgment, however, the district court granted Suzuki's motion based on its reading of Stroman. The district court held that "[t]he mutual release constitutes a knowing waiver of all claims under the [ADEA] notwithstanding the fact that the release does not specifically refer to the Act."

It is not clear to us whether the district court interpreted Stroman as holding that a general release of "all claims" includes a waiver of an ADEA claim, without the necessity to show that such waiver was deliberate, knowing, and voluntary. As discussed above, Stroman requires that the record show that the employee deliberately intended to waive his or her ADEA rights. See id. at 461-62. Because the record does not demonstrate whether, in signing a release of "all claims," Parker deliberately intended to waive his ADEA claims, we must vacate the order granting summary judgment and remand for the development of additional evidence, if such exists, regarding whether Parker deliberately, knowingly, and voluntarily intended to waive his ADEA claims.

---

*

This disposition is not appropriate for publication and may not be cited to or by the courts of this circuit except as provided by 9th Cir.R. 36-3

Chapter Nineteen

The 8th Circuit Court of Appeals ruling in Stevens

In the summer of 2001, while helping a family member do some research related to a criminal matter I discovered an Eighth Circuit Court of Appeals case, *Stevens v. McHan*, 3 F. 3d 1204, 1206 (1993), in which that court talked about reviewing district court's factual findings under the "clearly erroneous standard." In the above case the court stated,

> A factual finding is clearly erroneous if it is not supported by substantial evidence in the record, if it is based on an erroneous view of the law, or if the reviewing court is left with the definite and firm conviction that an error has been made.

This Circuit Court goes on to say,

> Findings supported by the record but based primarily on a trial judge's decision on the credibility of the witnesses can virtually never be clear error. Id. (quoting *Anderson*, 470 U.S. at 575, 105 S. Ct. at 1512, (1985).

I thought back to my case where the evidence showed that Judge Tanner made findings of intentional discrimination based primarily on the credibility of the witnesses and the evidence submitted during the trial. I then looked at the criteria set out by the Eighth Circuit Court of Appeals in *Stevens'* case related to a district court's factual findings under the clearly erroneous standard to see how their criteria fit with the ruling of the Ninth Circuit in my case. Since Judge Tanner made no factual findings on a waiver of my federal rights, how can a reviewing court determine that an erroneous view of the law has occurred? How could the reviewing court be left with the definite and firm conviction that an error has been made, when the Ninth Circuit admits that there were no oral testimonies from either party pertaining to a waiver of federal rights during the trial?

Additionally, the Eighth Circuit states in the *Stevens'* case,

> Under our standard of review, this court may not make an
> independent determination of the facts and reverse simply
> because it might have decided the case differently.

The standard of review is different between the Eighth Circuit Court of Appeals and the Ninth Circuit Court of Appeals. In the Ninth Circuit Court of Appeals, judges are able to reverse and dismiss a case without any oral testimony from the parties, and without any actual evidence on the record related to the reversal. Additionally, my case shows that some judges on the Ninth Circuit Court of Appeals are allowed to reverse an intentional racial employment discrimination case simply because the judges might have decided the case differently from the district court judge. All of the above is exactly what happened in my case. Any person, in my situation, would also have to wonder why he/she was treated so blatantly different than any other case mentioned in this story (specifically pertaining to whether or not it is the district court judge who decides if a valid waiver exists) by a federal appellate court. Moreover, based on this blatantly different treatment a federal appellate court reversed a federal district judge's ruling that I had proven that I was a victim of intentional racial employment discrimination.

Chapter Twenty

Double Standard for Employment Discrimination Cases

In 2002, while doing some research on employment discrimination, just to keep informed on this subject, I read a study published on the internet by two Cornell Law School Professors by the names of Theodore Eisenberg and Stewart J. Schwab. The study is called "Double Standard on Appeal: An Empirical Analysis of Employment Discrimination Cases in the U.S. Courts of Appeals." It is dated July 16, 2001.

These professors reviewed data from the Administrative Office of the United States Courts on the process of employment discrimination cases, through the federal appeal courts compared to other federal cases from 1988-1997.[62]

The study explains that cases begin in federal trial courts, called "district courts." The study states that whenever a case is filed in the federal district court, a form is filled out containing the basic information about the case including what type of claim it is. After this, the district court clerk files this form with the Administrative Office of the U.S. Courts. Once these forms are received by this federal office, they are,

> Assembled by the Federal Judicial Center and disseminated by the Inter-University Consortium for Political and Social Research. The purpose of this data collection is to provide an official public record of the business of the federal courts.

---

[62] This includes race, sex, and other discrimination claims filed under Title VII of the Civil Rights Act of 1964, age discrimination claims filed under the Age Discrimination in Employment Act, and disability claims filed under the Americans with Disabilities Act.

The study states,

> Since 1988, the Administrative Office has recorded the
> underlying district court docket number on all appellate
> cases. This has allowed us to link the district court and
> appellate cases and examine how cases fare on appeal.
> It is important to emphasize the data for this report comes
> from official government statistics covering all cases in
> the federal courts. It covers all decisions of the courts,
> not just the published decisions, so this data gives the
> best available overview of the activities of the United
> States courts.

From the information gathered by these two law professors
they concluded that "employment discrimination plaintiffs fared
dramatically worse than employers (defendants) on appeals." The
data show that the reversal rate when a plaintiff won at the federal
district court level in an employment discrimination case was
"greater than any other category of cases except other civil rights
cases". On the other hand, the reversal rate when an employer
(defendant) won at the federal district court level in an employment
discrimination case was smaller "than any other category of cases
except prisoner habeas corpus trials." The study states,

> The gap in reversal rates between discrimination plaintiffs
> and defendants (employers) in their trial judgments is
> astounding. The gap between defendants' and plaintiffs'
> success on appeal is larger in discrimination trials than
> in any other category of case, including civil prisoner
> cases.

The report also concluded that for cases that were decided at summary judgment level in favor of the plaintiff the *reversal rates for appellate review were similar to the reversal rate of plaintiff trial victories*. The report goes on to say it would seem that once a plaintiff has convinced a district court judge of the employer's wrongful intent that the findings (if there were findings made by the district court judge) of the district court judge would not be so easily overturned on appeal by the appellate court. Since the plaintiff survived all of the pretrial motions (i.e. summary judgment) leading to trial, this demonstrates that the plaintiff's allegations must not be frivolous, and shows that there are genuine issues of fact that need to be decided by the district court judge. There is no explanation for the rate of appellate court reversals in employment discrimination cases based on the study's findings.

The conclusion of this study states,

> The official data of the United States Courts reveal that employment discrimination plaintiffs fare miserably on appeal, and the dramatic gap in reversal rates in employment discrimination cases is a nationwide phenomenon, because it exists for all circuits throughout the country. The gap raises the specter that appellate courts have a double standard for employment cases, scrutinizing employee victories at trial while gazing benignly at employer victories at trial.

Unfortunately, the study did not divide the different categories of discrimination (i.e. race—mainly black plaintiffs, sex—mainly female plaintiffs, age—mainly older white male plaintiffs, or disability plaintiffs) so that one could investigate further which category does the best or worst on appeal.

I added this study to my story because my case was at the federal appellate court level during the period included in the data captured by the above-mentioned study. This study also gives credence to my allegations about the injustice carried out by two judges of the Ninth Circuit Court of Appeals.[63] My case shows that a U.S. Federal Appellate Court of Appeals will even fabricate lies to set aside a district court judge's ruling in favor of a racial employment discrimination plaintiff.

The information contained in the above study needs to be told to the public. Anyone who is covered by Title VII will know that besides facing discrimination in the workplace by the employer, there is a good chance that one will also endure discrimination at the federal appellate level, if fortunate enough to win at the district court level. Sure, no one could have known (I think) that an appellate court panel would fabricate lies in a published racial employment discrimination case to enforce this double standard, but my case shows that this can and did happen. If I was not assertive in exercising my civil rights, no one would have known that somehow federal appellate court judges have the power to commit frauds in a racial employment discrimination case, and possibly other cases, to achieve any particular outcome in any case that they desire. None of my attorneys spoke out publicly against the Ninth Circuit relating to the injustice that is reported at 884 F.2d 458 (*Stroman v. West Coast Grocery*). Perhaps this is

---

[63]   Also, see "How Employment Discrimination Plaintiff Fare in Federal Court," by Kevin M. Clermont and Stewart J. Schwab. Cornell Law faculty Publication—Journal of Empirical Legal Studies, Volume 1, Issue 2, 451-456 (Anti-Plaintiff Effect), July 2004.

because they fear retaliation by the Ninth Circuit should they have to present another case in front of this circuit.

Based on this double standard, I was deprived (meaning it is possible that any other citizen could be as well) the constitutional right to an impartial review of the actual district court's trial findings at the appellate court level. Since this was not afforded to me, these two government agents seriously injured my family and me. I have shown that an "oppressive wrong" was committed by these three judges (meaning my constitutional right to an impartial review was crushed by the abuse of authority exercised by these three judges) by not stating the truth. The truth is that there were no written findings of fact by the trial court judge relating to a waiver of my federal rights for an appellate court to review. Due to the fact that these three judges in their separately published decisions relating to my case neglected to tell the truth, I was denied an impartial review.

Lastly, from the "official government data collected from the Administrative Office of the United States Courts" pertaining to the federal courts, I may not be the only employment discrimination plaintiff who had their right to an impartial review by an appellate court violated due to the double standard by the appeal courts. However, I am probably the only employment discrimination plaintiff who was diligent enough to prove, and show to the public that some federal appellate court judges will fabricate lies in a case that is being reviewed by them in order to achieve the judgment that they desire for an employer.

Chapter Twenty-One

The Price I Paid for Fighting for My Rights

A little over a year after the U.S. Supreme Court refused to hear both of my petitions, in **February of 1993**, Cheryl and I separated. Before our separation, during the years that Cheryl was supporting the family, most of the time all four of us—Cheryl, our sons and I, were happy. We did things together like going to California to visit with family; going to places like Disneyland and the San Diego Zoo; camping and having barbecues with friends, and many activities in which the boys were involved.

Prior to this time, Cheryl was supportive of me in my struggle against WCG, although I do not believe she fully understood what I was going through. During the time period following Judge Tanner's decision in my favor, and prior to the Ninth Circuit Court of Appeals making their fraudulent ruling, WCG made offers to me to settle my case against them. Cheryl would help me interpret federal case laws pertaining to waivers of federal rights so I could make an informed decision regarding WCG's settlement offers. I researched federal case law, because my attorney wanted me to settle. He believed that the Ninth Circuit was not going to let me win, even though he could not point to any legal reason, or federal case law stating that I should not win. I told Cheryl that I would not settle based only on the fact that I am black, and she was in agreement with me.

In fact, my attorney had a meeting with Cheryl and me. I think he thought that he could convince Cheryl that I should take the settlement offer of $100,000.00, but Cheryl told him if he could not show us any legal reason why I should settle then she would stand by my decision. I then told my attorney if the Ninth Circuit Court of Appeals was going to overturn Judge Tanner's ruling in my case based on Judge Tanner and my race, then let them do it. After that, Cheryl, our sons, and I left my attorney's office.

After the Ninth Circuit Court of Appeals made their fraudulent ruling, Cheryl again helped me interpret the case law cited by the Ninth Circuit relating to my case. We both saw that the federal case law cited by the Ninth Circuit did not apply to the facts in my case. We both saw that none of the cases cited by the Ninth Circuit involved a plaintiff who won at a summary judgment level pertaining to an allegation of a waiver of federal rights, and in particular, a waiver of Title VII Rights. Furthermore, none of the cases cited addressed the fact that after a summary judgment decision was made in favor of the plaintiff and the case went to trial during which the federal district court judge refused to allow the same issues (which he already decided at the summary judgment level) to enter into the trial court record. When I was preparing a brief for a petition that I submitted to the U.S. Supreme Court concerning the actions by the Ninth Circuit Court of Appeals in my case, Cheryl proofread it for clarity before I gave it to Professor Rudolph to review to ensure it met the requirements for the U.S. Supreme Court. He said it did, and the U.S. Supreme Court accepted my petition.

The whole experience of standing up for my rights under the 1964 Civil Rights Act was starting to take a toll on me financially, and in my belief in the federal judicial system. I had to sell my 1981 Harley-Davidson Sportster motorcycle to help pay for bills while waiting for the appeal process. Because of the fraudulent ruling by the Ninth Circuit, I could not pay my back mortgage payments, which cost me my house and my Veteran Affairs (V.A.) housing entitlement. Then I had to sell my 1956 Chevy Nomad sport wagon that I had owned since 1973 to pay for the printing and filing of my writ of certiorari to the U.S. Supreme Court, which unfortunately they refused to hear. Eventually my belief in the federal judicial system started to take a toll on my relationship with Cheryl. It seemed to me that after the U.S. Supreme Court refused to hear my last petition, sometimes when Cheryl talked to me, I heard disrespect and contempt in her voice, for my leaving WCG.

One night our life together ended when Cheryl called the police to our home after we were arguing and told them that I had beaten her, which I strongly denied. What actually happened that night was Cheryl came into our bedroom where I was watching T.V. and she started telling me to put the boys to bed because they had fallen asleep with her in the front room watching T.V. I remember telling her that she should not tell me what to do, that she could put them to bed, or let them stay in the front room asleep since it was Friday night. For whatever reason, this grew into an argument between both of us, and she started hitting me. I admit that I did push her, and she hit the bedroom wall. I told her to leave me alone. She left the room, and I continued to watch T.V. until I fell asleep.

Two white Pierce County Sheriffs later awakened me and told me that Cheryl had made a report to the Sheriff's Office saying that I had beaten her. I just laughed when one of the officers told me about this accusation. I told them that she started hitting first, which caused me to push her off me, and then I told her to leave me alone and went back to watching T.V. One of the officers said he did not see any marks on me showing that she hit me. I responded by saying, "There were no marks on Cheryl showing that I had beaten her either." There was also no evidence from the house to show that there was a fight between Cheryl and me. The boys were in their beds asleep. I was asleep, and so I told them, "I don't know what she or you are talking about."

The two white sheriff's officers and Cheryl started talking to each other at the foot of the bed. When I saw this, I said, "I see what is going to happen now—since all three of you are white, my black ass is going to jail to make Cheryl happy." Then one of the white sheriff's officers said, "Yes, you are going to jail." While they were putting the handcuffs on me, I woke my sons up from sleeping so that they would see what was happening and told them "see what your mother is doing." Cheryl knew that I believed that the justice system is racist, not only because of my case against WCG, but from the many documented T.V. programs that we had watched together over the years. Now she had me, another black man involved with this racist judicial system. Since I am a black male, is the reason why I strongly believed I had to spend the weekend in jail since there was no evidence to show that either one of us had hit the other.

The following Monday, at the arraignment, I entered a not guilty plea. When my case went to court, the prosecuting attorney wanted me to have an anger evaluation before the case went any further, for which I had to pay. So I was ordered by the court to attend anger management classes that are set up through the Pierce County District Court. I went to one class where I first had to fill out an evaluation sheet concerning any anger issues that I may have before the class began. The class consisted of a group of ten men who were there by the order of the court pertaining to domestic violence, and a counselor who directed the class. Each of the men in the group described how they had handled an angry situation, which happened to them the week before coming to the class. After listening to each of their stories, it came to be my turn. I said to the counselor, "I do not have an anger problem and just because the court ordered me here does not mean that I have an anger problem." I then told the group, and counselor, about my experience with racial employment discrimination, and about my belief that because my wife is white, I was arrested. The

counselor then asked the group what they thought about what I
had just said. There were three blacks in the group, who said that
they could understand my stress, and frustration, if what I said was
true. The majority of whites in the group could not believe that the
white judges would lie, or that the white sheriff's officers arrested
me based on me being black. This example, in this group of nine
individuals, shows how blacks and whites view the legal system
differently. Here blacks could understand how my experiences
with racial employment discrimination and the situation with my
wife could cause my stress, and frustration, as a black man in a
racist society. However, on the other hand, the white individuals
could not accept or believe that the judicial system is discriminatory
or racist, or understand how this could lead to any frustration, or
stress, that I may be experiencing. This comparison showed me,
that there is still a division among the races, on how this nation's
justice is applied, and the affect it has on the views of individuals
of different races in this society.

I then asked the counselor if there was a black counselor, with
whom I could discuss my stress and frustration. I told him that if
I have an anger problem, it is from being a black man in a racist
society, and that he is not **black enough** or **experienced enough**
to counsel me on this problem. He said that in Pierce County there
are no black counselors involved with the courts, so I told him I
was not paying another $30.00 for something, or to someone,
who cannot understand my needs. The counselor wrote back to
the court and told the judge what I had said to him, and the judge
was angry with me. Nevertheless, the evaluation I completed did
not show that I had an anger problem. After a few months had
gone by since my arrest, and a few court appearances, the court
dismissed the case with prejudice. "Dismissed with prejudice"

means that based on the merits of the case the judge ruled that the case is over and no future action can come from this instance. The damage was already done between Cheryl and me, as far as I was concerned.

In April of 1997, Cheryl and I finally divorced, however, throughout the years following this incident I remain a part of my sons' lives. Now that both of them are in their twenties, they both tell me that they now understand why I left and understand why it was hard for me to go back to their mother. Both of them also said that when they were younger, they were confused and angry at me about the aforementioned incident. To me, the most important statement they made to me was when they both said that they love both of their parents and that both of them are happy and glad with the relationship that I have with each one of them. Despite the previous situations, I was happy to know that I did not lose my sons' love.

I am glad that over the years Cheryl and I were mature enough, for the love of our sons, to remain civil to each other. However, I do regret that it cost me so much to fight for rights that were denied to me—rights that I believed were guaranteed to all citizens of this nation, and particularly after I proved in federal district court that I was a victim of intentional racial discrimination.[64] I am concerned mainly about how this fight affected my two sons, Elijah and Tobias, especially my oldest son, Elijah.

The following is what Elijah stated to me during a conversation I had with him in 2009, after he read a draft of this story that I sent to him while he was incarcerated. He stated that he remembers

---

[64]   As I stated earlier this fight, cost me my family, my house, my V.A. housing benefits, my 1956 Chevrolet Nomad sport wagon that I had since graduating from high school, and a lot of mental stress.

that Aaron (because over the years Mr. Lee had become a close
friend of the family we refer to him by his first name—Aaron) and
I were always talking about WCG.

> Before mom and you separated, I remember Tobi and I
> having to go with you to the law library on many occasions
> and having to sit in the law library quietly while you did
> whatever you were doing. I remember having to go to
> Professor Rudolph's office and sit quietly during the
> lengthy and frequent visits while both of you talked about
> WCG and the Ninth Circuit.

He also mentioned remembering the many nights that both he and
Tobi could not bother me because I was typing all night until the
early morning hours—sometimes continuously 24 hours straight.
He and Tobi did not understand what I was typing, but now he
knows it was my brief to the U.S. Supreme Court and letters to
members of Congress. He did not know what was going on then
because he was so young, but now after reading my manuscript
he understands what I was going through.

Elijah also expressed his admiration for me when considering
all that I have been through—from the time of my mother's
passing, to beating the odds of staying out of the judicial system,
to furthering my education, and most importantly, to standing
up for what I believe is right. He told me that he remembers my
college graduation party that his mother had for me after I received
my bachelor's degree, and how proud the family was of me, and
how his mother's friends and my friends were happy for me and
congratulating me all night as we all danced and laughed.

He stated,

I do remember before mom and you separated that both
of you did argue a lot, and when mom got mad at you, you
were the one running away from her or locking yourself
in the bathroom until she calmed down.

Now that he is older and has an adult perspective on domestic
relations between a man and a woman, he does not believe I beat
his mother the way she told everyone at that time. He went on to
state that he had seen women who had been beaten by their men,
and in comparison, he never witnessed a mark on his mom during
the years that we were together.

He knows now if the Ninth Circuit would not have lied and would
have held WCG accountable, the undue amount of stress in our
household would not have led to mom and me separating, and
ripping the family apart. He stated he believes his life would have
been different if the Ninth Circuit Court of Appeals would not have
committed the fraud against me. The stress that he witnessed came
from me fighting WCG, and the Ninth Circuit Court of Appeals,
and made his parents stop loving each other. Afterward he lost
(his father) the only person who could discipline him, teach him
how to stay out of trouble, and to become a responsible man.
Because of the action by the Ninth Circuit, which he heard about
while he was with me at Professor Rudolph's office and through my
conversations with Aaron, he lost respect and trust in the justice
system. Elijah stated,

I do not think I would have spent so many years in the
juvenile system if my parents were then together. While
I was in the juvenile system, I knew that you kept asking
the court to give custody of me to you. The court kept

sending me back to mom because, as they stated, "They did not want to separate the household." But that was exactly what they were doing each time they locked me up after I kept getting into trouble while living with mom. Now, dad, I recognized what you were going through with the court when you were asking white judges to do something that mom did not want done, which was to give you custody of me.

I then stopped him and told him, I admit I was running the streets like your mother told the court. I told the court I was a single black man stripped of my employment based on my race, and stripped of my federal judgment in my Title VII case against my ex-employer by the Ninth Circuit Court of Appeals based on my race. I told the court, "Now all I have are my sons and I could save Elijah if the court gave me custody of him." I told the court that both Elijah's parents love him. Elijah stated,

> Dad, I know mom loved me so much, that she would not give custody to you and the court always agreed with her. Now the result is like you stated would happen—that the juvenile system will groom me for prison life if custody is not changed. Now I am in prison for a long time. And I remember you telling me, and the court, *that this is where my son will be if the court won't allow me custody of him.*

The last thing Elijah told me during this conversation was that I needed to tell this story because an injustice was done to me, but also that this injustice effected him. "So if you are going to tell this story, tell it all, so whoever reads it will get the full effect of what happened to you, me, and to our family."

After Elijah's and my conversation I thought to myself, "maybe if I had only wanted to be an order selector my son would not be where he is today? If only I would have *stayed in my place*, as it had been told to blacks throughout the history of this nation, I might have been able to save my oldest son from being a statistic." It has taken me over eighteen years to finally find a job that is equal to the pay and benefits I was receiving at WCG. Now looking back, considering all that I have lost, I sometimes wonder, was it worth thinking that I would receive the same rights as whites, at a white owned corporation, when it comes to the judicial system?

I have learned, and hope that my story has illustrated to you, the reader, that the struggle for this nation to overcome the existing institutional racism in the judicial system continues. Additionally, the silence of the entire Ninth Circuit Court of Appeals and the U.S. Supreme Court makes them accomplices in the frauds committed by these two federal appellate judges. It should be an outrage that innocent parties had to suffer because judges will commit lies (frauds) based upon racism; that judges will manipulate the outcome of a trial judge's summary judgment decision, manipulate established federal case law, and violate a federal civil procedure rule, to achieve a ruling that they wanted. It is especially outrageous when the actions of these two federal appellant judges were outside their judicial capacity according to Federal Civil Procedure Rule 52, and U.S. Supreme Court case law, where their action negatively affected my life and the life of my innocent family.

Chapter Twenty-Two

The History of the Black Military Personnel

It is an insult to all the black military service personnel, who were willing to fight, and died, for the rights and freedoms for all U.S. citizens, that in 1989 after a black military personnel gets out of the military he/she cannot enjoy all of these rights and freedoms in a federal appellate court. In particular, it would seem black military personnel have paid a heavy price to be able to enjoy the rights and freedoms contained in the Constitution as a U.S. citizen (such as due process). In fact, Michael Eric Dyson (who is an author and radio host) states,

> Since the time of slavery, blacks have actively defended the U.S. in every war it has waged, from the Civil War down to the war on terrorism, a loyalty to the Federal Government conceived by black leaders as a critical force in gaining freedom [65].

Mr. Dyson goes on to say,

> W.E.B. Dubois argued in World War I that blacks should forget our special grievances and close our ranks with our white fellow citizens. Some 380,000 soldiers answered the call even as they failed to reap the benefits of their sacrifices when they came home.

In addition, historically many blacks have stated, they believed by going into the military, to defend the U.S., and the Constitution, and

---

[65] In an article entitled "Understanding Black Patriotism," dated Thursday April 24, 2008, that was published in Times Magazine dated May 5, 2008.

through their sacrifices, that they would be entitled to the same rights, benefits, and freedom as white citizens.

With the above in mind, I tell the reader, I thought by the 1980's, I would reap the benefits guaranteed within the Constitution and which so many black veterans, like myself, believed would come to them by going into the military. I thought someone would be concerned about my allegations of a disingenuous ruling by these two appellate court judges, which denied this veteran his Constitutional Right to due process to have the *November 1, 1985 document* litigated at the trial court level, if needed.

I know some individuals may wonder why I continue to keep this fight going. I would say to them that I am willing to keep on fighting for the rights and freedoms contained in the Bill of Rights and the Fourteenth Amendment to the Constitution for several reasons. First, I am a citizen. Second, I am a veteran of this great nation who was willing to fight and die for those rights. Third, these two Ninth Circuit judges intentionally harmed me, due to my race.[66]

Lastly, I read an article written by Sandi Doughton entitled "Fort Lawton vet dies hours after apology," which was reported in the Seattle Times Newspaper on **July 28, 2008**. The article stated how a Washington State Congress member pressed for a review of a court-martial of 27 black soldiers that took place over 60 years ago, for a brawl in which an Italian prisoner was killed in the Seattle area. Even though this incident was tried in a military

---

[66] From the Booker T. Washington's book I remember this quote, ". . . people are usually surprised if the Negro boy does not fail . . . the Negro youth starts out with the presumption against him." I want to show that I did not fail, I over came this presumption, and I was intentionally harmed by the Ninth Circuit Court of Appeals because of my race.

court, it shows that a Congress member can look into a case to find out if any individual's constitutional rights were violated. The Congressperson did this knowing that in order to review a court-martial trial court's records that involved 27 soldiers, who were found guilty of a killing, would be a very time consuming operation. Nonetheless, this Washington State Congress member pressed the Army for a review of the court-martial against these black soldiers and afterwards the Army apologized for the "grievous wrong" done to these 27 soldiers more than sixty years ago.

Even though my case was a civil case and not a criminal case, a Congress member should have the same power to press for a review of the federal court trial records, especially to see if allegations of fraud by two appellate court judges did in fact deprive a citizen (veteran) of his constitutional right to due process. If finding out the truth is really an important issue in a court-martial, then it should also be an important issue involving a racial employment discrimination civil case. It seems that an ex-soldier that was involved with a civil rights case should have the same right to truth and justice as a group of ex-soldiers wrongly convicted in a court-martial case, or individuals who have been wrongly convicted in a criminal case. The evidence contained in this book surely shows that more than twenty years ago, two appellate court judges committed lies (frauds) to set aside findings against a major white owned corporation. It would seem if the integrity of two appellate judges were in question, then someone would look into the allegations against them, since it is integrity that judges are assumed to have. I hope that if justice ever comes in my case it will be before **"I'm in my deathbed."**

My Conclusion

Now that you have read my story, I want to state when I have weighed the good against the bad, overall I am proud of myself. The totality of this experience has made me a stronger individual with more self-confidence. An ordeal like this one could have broken many individuals, but I survived with my self-pride and dignity.[67]

However, on a number of occasions, I have been asked, "If I had to do this over again, would I have done and do the same thing," and I say yes. "If I could change anything, it would be to not expose my sons, especially my oldest son, at such an early age to the racism and discrimination rhetoric." I would have also fought harder to get custody of my oldest son. Not that I love one more than the other, but because I now know that I was the only person who could have saved him from spending all of his teenage years in and out of this state juvenile system, and ending up where he is now.

My feelings are that I have written a true story. A story that has been told by many Black Americans throughout the history of this nation. A story about how Black Americans have been shown that they do not have the same rights and privileges, which are

---

[67] Also, from the "Up From Slavery" book, I read this quote ". . . out of the hard and unusual struggle through which he (the Negro youth) is compelled to pass, he gets a strength, a confidence, that one misses whose pathway is comparatively smooth by reason of birth and race." Over the years, I realized how much this quote applies to me. However, my struggles fighting for my rights have shown me this nation's legal system is based on race.

supposed to be guaranteed by federal law. Also, just because an individual puts on a black robe does not mean that an individual has the integrity to wear that robe in all situations.[68]

Now that I have told you what this American citizen/veteran did, I ask you, as an American, *"What would you have done? Would you have spoken out against the discriminatory work environment, or would you have just been quiet and accepted the discriminatory work environment?"* The above would also apply to the *untruthful and racist* ruling by the Ninth Circuit Court of Appeals surrounding my case.

---

[68] In a book entitled "Black Robes, White Justice" written by New York Supreme Court Justice Bruce Wright, he contends that ". . . most judges—male, white and middle class—currently have no understanding of racism or its influence on their thinking and conduct." However, in my case these two judges knew exactly how their racism influence their thinking and conduct pertaining to their ruling.

Epilogue

I want my sons to know my life before they were born, the obstacles that I had to overcome, which in some ways helped me to become the proud black man that I am. I especially wanted them to know about the discrimination that I experienced at WCG, and the injustice that is still within the judicial system, based on race. Furthermore, I want them to know that to combat this racism one must never stop educating oneself and have the faith in oneself that one can overcome this obstacle if it is put it in front of them.

From my story they will know that despite all I have been through I have never stopped educating myself, never stopped believing that I could make it through any situation, or that I am less than anyone else. Sure, the actions by WCG and these two federal circuit judges de-valued me as a man and a veteran for awhile, but they never completely de-valued my self worth, or my dignity. I realize that standing up for my right to be treated equal put me in a category with Rosa Parks, when she refused to give up her seat on the bus. It put me in a category with Congressman Adam Clayton Powell who refused the practice of Black Congressmen not being permitted to eat with White Congressmen in the Congressional dining facility; or with James Meredith who demanded and got the rights properly extended to any white citizen wanting to attend the University of Mississippi; and the students in their nonviolent and respectful lunch counter sit-ins. These individuals, as well as Dr. King, were probably called militant, or other such names, by both black and white citizens because they refused to accept the theory that black citizens do not have the same rights and privileges as white citizens.

From my struggles for equal employment opportunities and equal treatment from the Federal Appellate Court for the Ninth Circuit, I want my sons, and anybody else to know, to never stop fighting to be treated as equal to any other citizen in this country. Hopefully, the truth and justice pertaining to my case will come before I die, so that I may see it. If not, maybe someone who reads my story will continue my fight after I am gone, for the truth and justice, that should have been reported by the Ninth Circuit in their published ruling in the Federal Reporter in volume 884 F.2d on page 462. Also, maybe someone will speak out against this lie (fraud) created by these two appellate judges that was motivated by race. Most of all, I want my sons to know, from all of my life experiences, a quote, which I have always kept in my mind that I read by Dr. Martin Luther King where he stated, "The ultimate measure of a man is not where he stands in moments of comfort and convenience, but where he stands in times of challenges and controversies." I believe my stance through my life challenges and controversies has shown my sons "how I measure as a man."

Testimonials

Although the intent of Title VII of the 1964 Civil Rights Act was to eliminate discrimination in the workplace, there are several areas within the congressionally established system (e.g. EEOC operations at the local level, such as state HRCs contracted to perform investigations) where this intent fails to result in the desired outcome (i.e. elimination of discrimination in the workplace). Unfortunately, in many cases, it adds to the levels of bureaucracy through which an individual must navigate, as well as the additional documentation and procedures an individual must provide and follow in order to make a claim. These additional burdens have jaded the majority of those familiar with the system to the point that the rallying cry among lawyers, legal authorities, academics, etc. is "take the settlement!" Yet, 'settling' does nothing to improve poor work conditions! Meanwhile, it silences those best equipped to offer suggestions about possible remedies, and encourages organizations and companies that engage in such practices to continue doing so.

Even more disturbing than the shortcomings of Congress at the local level, is the fact that those who have had the gumption to pursue a case to the federal level (against all advice to settle) have not been supported in the federal appellate courts. Stroman's efforts are just one example among many. The major difference between Stroman and others who have faced such challenges is that he refused to be silenced. His story is worth reading and sharing with everyone else who expects the court system to protect his/her Constitutional rights.

Sefla Fuhrman
August 2012

This was a journey by Mr. Stroman, through the Washington State Human Rights Commission, a Federal District Court, U.S. Court of Appeals, and various other institutions. In which he was trying to receive a positive judgment surrounding his allegations of intentional racial employment discrimination by his then employer. The narrative should be interesting, informative, quite inspiring to some, to say the least.

It would seem to me, although I am certainly no expert, that there is more than adequate documentation produced by him in his book, to support his desire to write an account of his experience at the appeals court. The documents clearly show to a reasonable person, that the system did not work properly pertaining to his case. More importantly, the exhibits show what is reported by the appeals court, is not genuine.

Moreover, and being a veteran myself, knowing that military personnel are sworn to defend Constitutional rights. I understand why Mr. Stroman, also a veteran, was disappointed and hurt. All of the above institutions except the federal district court, showed that they would not recognize, or enforce, his right to due process.

Dale Harter
March 2012

Another Cries for Justice
Grady Michael Stroman

This is a compelling true story of a struggle for justice.
Michael's core values are established at an early age by the
strength, courage and faith of his mother. While still a
teenager he suffers the most devastating tragedy. The reader
cannot help but to be moved by the gripping, heart-wrenching,
emotionally charged account of the tragedy. Michael is not
made bitter, but rather emerges with a resolve and
determination to continue his mother's legacy.

Throughout Michael's early life he is immersed in a harmonious
multicultural society, so it comes as a shock when he
experiences racial discrimination in the workplace. He attempts
to rectify the situation but is rebuked again and again until he
finally finds it necessary to file a lawsuit.

The discrimination was so blatant; Michael's case readily won,
only to be overturned by the Ninth Circuit Court of Appeals,
which I don't fully understand because Michael had jumped
through all the hoops, and consistently sought justice through
all the proper channels. I believe this case is definitely a
miscarriage of justice.

Ruth Asare
September, 2011

The saying "Walk a Mile in my Shoes" comes to mind when I think of Michael. Most people would turn out bitter and hateful having lived his life, but he has not allowed that to happen to him.

He has survived incredible tragedy, in the way he lost his Mother. She instilled in him a tenacious sprit when it came to equal rights and justice. He used the tenacity to win his case against a company that clearly discriminated against him, only to be let down by the same system who told him he was RIGHT!

Read Michael's story and you will be shocked to learn the prejudice discrimination and corruption still rampant within our society and especially the judicial system

Kimber Dale